THE HIRE ADVANTAGE™

A Proven Approach to Overcoming Today's Job Search Challenges

Greg Wood, CCMP

Adapted from the four books in
TheHireAdvantage™ Job Search Series

www.TheHireChallenge.com

PETERSON'S

THE HIRE ADVANTAGE™

A Proven Approach to Overcoming Today's
Job Search Challenges

by Greg Wood, CCMP

 **PETERSON'S**

About Peterson's

Peterson's provides the accurate, dependable, high-quality education content and guidance you need to succeed. No matter where you are on your academic or professional path, you can rely on Peterson's print and digital publications for the most up-to-date education exploration data, expert test-prep tools, and top-notch career success resources—everything you need to achieve your goals.

For more information, contact Peterson's, 3 Columbia Circle, Suite 205, Albany, NY 12203-5158; 800-338-3282 Ext. 54229; or find us online at www.petersonsbooks.com.

Bernadette Webster, Managing Editor; Ray Golaszewski, Publishing Operations Manager; Linda M. Williams, Composition Manager

ISBN-13: 978-0-7689-3790-9

Printed in the United States of America

10 9 8 7 6 5 4 3 2 1   15 14 13

Also available for military veteran job seekers is TheHireTactics™ book series.

Welcome to my best-selling series on the new job-search reality. This book is a combination of four best-selling books that are dedicated to helping people like you succeed in your job search. The four different sections of this book are designed to be short and sweet so you can quickly begin using this proven job search approach. All four books are available as ebooks through both Amazon.com and BarnesandNoble.com.

Section 1—PACKAGING YOU!

Every job seeker uses a resume and a cover letter. But to actually secure a job you need to do more. This section introduces you to the tools you need to brand yourself so you can separate yourself from your competition.

Section 2—FIRE YOUR RESUME!

Don't let your job search turn into Clicking, Reviewing, Applying, and Praying, what we like to call C.R.A.P. In this section you'll learn the strategies and techniques that can help you penetrate the hidden job market by broadcasting your value to the business community and not your need for a "job." You'll also learn how to convince employers that you are the solution to their problems and more than just what's on a piece of paper with antiquated formatting.

Section 3—52 JOB INTERVIEW QUESTIONS YOU NEED TO KNOW!

Once you use my packaging tools to set you apart from the crowd, you can use my advice on interviewing to "seal the deal." Preparation is key and this section teaches you how to demonstrate the value you bring to the table, which will greatly enhance your opportunity to win the job offer.

Section 4—NEGOTIATING YOUR TRUE WORTH

If you've been out of work for some time, it can be tempting to accept the job offer as is and start the job right away. In this section you'll learn how to evaluate whether or not the job is worth taking and then how to negotiate the difference between what you're offered and your true worth to the organization.

ABOUT THE AUTHOR

Greg Wood, CCMP

Greg Wood is a Certified Career Management Professional (CCMP) who has experienced firsthand the challenges and anxiety of being unemployed several times during his 30-plus years of business experience. With more than 13 years of experience in both outplacement and executive search, Greg earned his reputation as a preeminent career counselor through the creation of TheHireRoad, an innovative, strategic approach to the job search. His unique program takes job seekers step-by-step through the entire job-search process, providing all the resources and tools necessary to achieve differentiation and shorten their time in transition at a very critical time in their lives.

An excellent trainer and presenter, Mr. Wood is a frequent guest speaker at a variety of professional and career transition support groups around the nation. In 2010, he was interviewed by talk show host Bill Handel on KFI AM640 radio in Los Angeles, one of the top news/talk shows in the country. Greg has also appeared on the "Job Seekers Clinic Show" on KFWB News Talk 980.

Greg's corporate background includes domestic and international experience in a variety of industries, including executive search, publishing, high technology, and health care. He has held senior management positions with mid-size as well as major Fortune 500 corporations.

To contact Greg for keynotes, corporate outplacement, and one-on-one consultation:

Greg Wood
TheHireChallenge
4340 E. Indian School Road, Suite 21
Phoenix, AZ 85018
Office: (602) 237-5366
E-mail: Greg@TheHireChallenge.com

For more information on TheHireRoad™ Job Search System:
http://www.TheHireChallenge.com

TESTIMONIALS

Here are just a few comments from job seekers who have taken TheHireRoad™ approach:

"I think TheHireRoad program should become part of the workforce development system as an added feature available in the One Stop Career Centers throughout the United States. I highly recommend this product."

Jim McShane
Public Administrator, Illinois (WIA)
Workforce Investment Act System

"I had the pleasure of meeting Greg about a month ago and learning about the job search strategies he teaches with TheHireRoad. In the space of those four weeks I have been actively applying TheHireRoad resources and strategy for communicating added value to potential employers. In that short time I received three invitations for interviews with hiring managers of companies I was most interested in!

This week I was offered a position at one of these companies which I gratefully accepted. Although the outcome speaks for itself, it was the process of getting there with Greg's help for which I am most THANKFUL. I appreciate that Greg not only gave me the resources, but he helped me to use them with the most impact. I am humbled and grateful for within four weeks of being suddenly unemployed, I have what looks like will be a great job."

Ron Sato
Santa Ana, California

"TheHireRoad™ was pivotal in my search for new employment, giving me all the professional tools necessary to maximize my employment search, prepare for interviews and create a post-interview presentation of myself, all of which enabled me to stand out from the competition and land the perfect job. I would recommend Greg and TheHireRoad™ to anyone who is looking to put all the integral pieces of a new employment search together."

Leslie Rush
Oceanside, California

"Greg is an excellent teacher and an inspirational role model. He is empowering while sharing his knowledge and motivates job seekers to test his unique techniques in real life. Greg has been a great supporter throughout the process, providing practical advice and hope. I highly recommend Greg's services to all on the road to success."

Klara Detrano
Costa Mesa, California

"TheHireRoad was very effective and helped shorten my time between jobs. The seminar is a welcome change from the standard advice found in numerous books and tapes, especially the approach to interviewing. I'm sure the strategies will be just as valuable if and when I find myself in transition again."

Larry Weimann
St. Louis, Missouri

"I did use TheHireRoad program. The CDs and the DVD were great. I have had three job offers, accepted one last week, and started Monday."

Jason Stone
Alpharetta, Georgia

"TheHireRoad really gave me the help I needed. I went into the interview with a lot of confidence and got the offer!"

Susan Cole
Indianapolis, Indiana

"TheHireRoad was an instrumental part of beginning my job search. The in-home seminar turned the anxiety of the interview into a position of knowledge and confidence. I am very happy to have made the choice to go with TheHireRoad and I have nothing but praise for their techniques, knowledge, and strategies."

Robert King
Whittier, California

"The techniques I learned with this program have helped me revitalize my job search and boost my confidence. Now I'm actually getting interviews!"

Donna Schowalter
Newport Beach, California

For more information visit: http://www.TheHireChallenge.com.

CONTENTS

About the Author v

Testimonials vi

SECTION 1   Packaging You!

Introduction: Welcome to the New Job Reality 3

Why TheHireAdvantage™ 3

The Four Milestones 4

Chapter One: Differentiation Is Critical 7

C.R.A.P. 8

Step 1—Selling Yourself 9

Step 2—Defining Your Value 11

Chapter Two: YOU Are the Product and YOU Are the Salesperson 17

Your Marketing Toolbox 19

Tool Number 1: Your 10-Second Commercial 19

Tool Number 2: Personal Business Cards 20

Tool Number 3: Resumes 22

Tool Number 4: The Biography 23

Tool Number 5: Cover Letters 24

Tool Number 6: Management Endorsements 25

Tool Number 7: The Post-Interview Packet 26

Tool Number 8: References 27

Additional Marketing Tools 28

Chapter Three: Creating a Resume and Cover Letter 29

The Chronological Resume 29

The Functional Resume 29

The Combination Resume 30

More You Should Know About Resumes 39

Sample Biography 41

Sample Strategic Value Letter 43

Sample Strategic Job Listing Letter. 44

Strategic Networking Letter 45

Strategic Meeting Letter 46

Strategic Referral Letter 47

Strategic Research Letter. 48

Summary 49

SECTION 2   Fire Your Resume!

Chapter Four: The "Traditional" Job Search Approach 53

Don't Waste Your Money! 54

Chapter Five: Four Reasons Not to Send a Resume 57

Reason 1—Resumes End Up in Human Resources 57

Reason 2—Resumes Are Used to Screen You Out 58

Reason 3—Resumes Are Not Value Propositions 59

Reason 4—Resumes Do Not Differentiate You. 59

Chapter Six: It's Time to Change Your Mindset! 61

Resource 1—Internal Candidates 62

Resource 2—Referral/Recommendations/Word-of-Mouth. 63

Resource 3—Posting a Job Opening 63

Resource 4—Hire a Recruiter 63

Chapter Seven: Tactics for a Successful Job Search in the New Economy . . . 65

Tactic #2—Target Companies, Not Jobs 65

Tactic #3—Define Your Value. 67

Tactic #4—Target the Hiring Manager 69

Tactic #5—Get Referred to the Hiring Manager. 70

Tactic #6—Broadcast Your Value, Not Your Resume 70

Tactic #7—Initiate a Dialog. 71

Chapter Eight: Using Social Networks in Your Job Hunt 77

An Introduction to LinkedIn 77

SECTION 3   52 Job Interview Questions You Need to Know!

Introduction. 89

Chapter Nine: 10 Steps for Preparing for Your Strategic Interview 93

Chapter Ten: Personal Questions 95

Chapter Eleven: Knowledge Questions 105

Chapter Twelve: Situational Questions. 109

Chapter Thirteen: Experience Questions. 113

Chapter Fourteen: Stress Questions. 119

Chapter Fifteen: Salary Questions 123

Chapter Sixteen: Questions YOU Need to Ask 125

Chapter Seventeen: Summary and Closing 129

SECTION 4   Negotiating Your True Worth!

Chapter Eighteen: They Made You a Job Offer! 133

You Got an Offer! 133

Acknowledging Your Offer 134

Job Types 135

Offer Components 135

Your Worth in the Marketplace 136

Chapter Nineteen: Key Considerations 139

    Be Prepared 139

    Key Considerations 139

    Cash Compensation 139

    Must-Haves 141

    Company Life Cycle 142

    What's Your Price? 143

Chapter Twenty: The Art of Negotiation 145

    Basis for Negotiation 145

    The Process of Negotiation 145

    Strategies to Negotiate a Higher Base Salary 147

    The Negotiation Discussion. 149

Chapter Twenty-One: Summary and Conclusion. 151

    Financial Analysis Worksheet 152

    Job Offer Component Checklist 157

    Your Analysis of Job Offer 159

    Closing Thoughts. 160

    TheHireRoad™ Job Search System. 163

APPENDIX

Glossary 167

SECTION 1

Packaging You!

INTRODUCTION

Welcome to the New Job Reality

Welcome to TheHireAdvantage™—our series presenting job search strategies and tactics for today's new job search environment!

The content in TheHireAdvantage series does not remotely resemble any of the information found in those self-help "for dummies" books. This book is not "A Complete Idiot's Guide" to job searching and does not contain easy-to-do tasks designed to get you a job in four easy steps or just "24 days." We make no such promises. This series is for job seekers who are frustrated, discouraged, and increasingly fed up and want answers and solutions, not clever book titles and unrealistic promises.

WHY TheHireAdvantage™

While there are many sources of job search information, they all focus on outdated traditional approaches that no longer work. Most job search books recycle information from the books that preceded them. They ARE NOT focusing on the new reality that resumes and human resources departments are barriers, not enablers, to you landing a job. You can pull a newspaper from the 1980s, 1990s or early 2000s and find the exact same information about resumes, cover letters, and wearing a nice suit.

The same is true for job search advice found on the Internet. All of it old, almost none of the information is new.

Things have changed.

Times have changed.

And times are tough.

YOU NEED NEW TOOLS AND NEW TACTICS FOR THIS NEW JOB REALITY.

Job search success in our new economy requires creativity, a willingness to think outside the box and innovative approaches to meet the challenges of finding employment.

Are you willing to change your mindset in order to succeed in today's fiercely competitive job market?

Are you willing to learn new techniques (new tactics and strategies) for the new job reality?

If so, read on!

THE FOUR MILESTONES

After hundreds of interviews with job seekers and a decade of working inside both large corporations and small businesses as a consultant, I discovered there are **Four Milestones to an effective job search:**

MILESTONE 1—Packaging: This milestone is all about using innovative marketing tools that clearly differentiate you from your competition. This is the focus of **SECTION 1** *Packaging You!* in this book.

MILESTONE 2—Promotion: To get a job, you need to educate the business community (hiring managers) by broadcasting your value, NOT your resume. This is the focus of **SECTION 2** *Fire Your Resume!* I discuss the innovative tools that job seekers need today to be successful in getting past human resources and in front of a hiring manager.

MILESTONE 3—Product Demonstration: The interview is the crux of your job search. To be successful and become the candidate of choice, you need to conduct a strategic interview versus a traditional interview. You need to explain to the hiring manager why you're the best candidate for the job. This is the subject of **SECTION 3,** *52 Job Interview Questions You Need to Know!,* our section on interviewing prepares you to conduct a strategic interview by supplying you with critical questions often asked in job interviews and suggested answers.

MILESTONE 4—Pricing: One of the most difficult challenges for job seekers is determining a fair offer for employment. **SECTION 4,** *Negotiating Your True Worth,* is where you'll negotiate the difference between what you're offered and your true worth to the organization.

So let's get started with MILESTONE 1—Packaging. You will learn more about the process and the marketing tools you'll need to clearly distinguish yourself so you can achieve job-search success!

CHAPTER ONE

Differentiation Is Critical

The main goal of the four milestones is to help you achieve **differentiation**. Differentiation is critical to ensure you stand out from the herd of other job applicants. If you do not standout or if you're not seen as the outstanding or preferred candidate, you are simply another commodity applicant.

One definition of commodity is:

A PRODUCT, SUCH AS FOOD, GRAINS, OR METALS, WHICH IS INTERCHANGEABLE WITH ANOTHER PRODUCT OF THE SAME TYPE. THE PRICE OF THE COMMODITY IS SUBJECT TO SUPPLY AND DEMAND.

Notice the key words **interchangeable** and **supply and demand**. If you do not differentiate yourself then you are interchangeable with every other candidate. In today's economy, there are far more job seekers than jobs. Depending on the job expertise required, there may be 100 to more than 5,000 applicants for a single job.

This means the supply of interchangeable job applicants greatly exceeds the jobs available. Under the law of supply and demand, when there is a lot of a commodity, the price (salary) falls.

So you do NOT want to be a commodity. You want to **stand out** from all other applicants and be perceived as the **outstanding** candidate. You want to be the one hired and for a value that is worthy of your experience and expertise.

Your goal is the word used at the start of this chapter—DIFFERENTIATION. In other words, how do you distinguish yourself from all other candidates? How do you separate yourself from all those people chasing the same jobs that you are pursuing?

The good news for you is virtually all job seekers follow the traditional approach to a job search that relies on want ads and Internet job boards. Desperate job seekers have been led to mistakenly believe that a powerful resume and a knock-'em-dead cover letter will get them in the door for an interview and in front of the hiring manager. However, this approach fails miserably. You will NOT be using those tactics!

C.R.A.P.

What many in the job search industry refer to as the traditional approach we call C.R.A.P.: **C**licking, **R**eviewing, **A**pplying, and **P**raying.

Millions of job applicants just like you spend their days clicking around the Internet on job boards, Craigslist, corporate websites, and maybe even reading the old-fashioned newspaper want ads. You review the descriptions and decide that maybe you are close enough for the position and decide to apply.

If you are an experienced job seeker, you may take a moment to customize your resume and cover letter to more closely match the job description. But eventually you will submit the same old resume that everyone else submits and pray the phone rings to set up an interview.

Sound familiar?

Have you done the same series of actions day in and day out?

If you have, I can guarantee you are getting the same result as all the other job seekers I counsel: **Nothing**.

You are simply adding your paperwork to a massive pile of identical resumes. And that assumes you get past the automated "meatgrinder" resume-scanning software that searches out special keywords and phrases that may or may not be on your resume.

We all know there has to be a better way.

When I was in your position, I knew I had a lot to offer an employer in terms of skills, experience, and expertise. But I needed to get noticed. I had to somehow stand out during every step of the job search process. I needed differentiation.

And so do you!

You need to determine how you are going to stand out to the employers with jobs you can do. And you do that in two steps: selling yourself and defining your value.

STEP 1—SELLING YOURSELF

The first step for job search success is to get comfortable with the idea of selling yourself (ouch!).

You MUST understand that you are seen by potential employers as one product among many (thousands upon thousands) in the job market. Success in your job search will mean convincing prospective employers to buy you instead of the other products (job applicants). You need to become "the one" who solves their problem and meets their needs.

YOU NEED TO
BECOME
THE ONE WHO
SOLVES THEIR
PROBLEM AND
MEETS THEIR NEEDS.

You need to take this information and create a winning sales pitch. In marketing terminology, this is called your "Unique Selling Proposition" or USP. A good USP will answer the question in the mind of every interviewer you'll meet in the job-search process, which is: Why should I hire you?

By the way, I have seen this step done so well by some job seekers that the hiring manager changed the job description to fit them instead of being measured against the original description! I have also seen applicants who were so well positioned that they created a job where one did not exist.

If you are not comfortable selling yourself, **Get over it!**

You need to be comfortable with who you are and what you can do to help the future employer. You need to be confident that you can do the job required. We know that selling yourself isn't easy. But you don't have to just depend upon your own opinion. You can use the positive endorsements of others to help sell you. One of the tools that works for my clients is the Management Endorsements.

Management Endorsements aren't references. Instead they're written praise from your former employers and managers. Usually these are found on your evaluations, which by law you are entitled to. You can lift direct quotes from your evaluations and put them together to create an endorsement listing that fully shows a potential employer why they should hire you. Here's an example:

BRUCE R. FIELD

MANAGEMENT ENDORSEMENTS

"Bruce has consistently demonstrated his ability to meet his sales performance objectives"

> Robert A. Spangler
> Vice President, Sales
> SunGard Corporation

"Bruce is always willing to go out of his way to work with new Sales Representatives and is a great team player"

> Richard M. Weber
> Sr. Vice President of Sales
> Cyborg Corporation

"Using his consultative approach with his clients has enabled Bruce to establish solid business relationships that have resulted in significant revenue generation to the Company"

> John M. Sharp
> Regional Sales Manager
> Pitney Bowes, Inc.

"Bruce is focused on providing our customers with the right solution. He takes great pride in his ethical and professional approach to his work, and is highly regarded by both the Company and our clients"

> Steven Michaels
> Regional Sales Manager
> Donnelley Enterprise Solutions

In **SECTION 3,** *52 Job Interview Questions You Need to Know,* there are 52 questions that you will likely be asked in an interview. Being familiar with those questions and rehearsing with a coach may be something you need to consider if selling yourself is a terrifying thought.

STEP 2—DEFINING YOUR VALUE

I know this may shock many readers but . . .

Employers do NOT want to hire employees!

Employees are expensive and in today's economy can become a liability and not an asset. So employers hire only when they must. They hire to solve problems and provide the services they need. By hiring you, the company is investing in your ability to address issues and solve problems that will lead to greater profitability. In other words, your value will far outweigh the cost to employ you.

So when you create your USP, think of it as a commercial that will define your **value to the business community and to the company that is hiring.** Your USP will explain why they need to "buy" you and your skills, and it will give employers a reason to see you as an asset. You have to make sure they understand that you can solve their problems.

I cannot emphasize this enough!

Whether you're just beginning your job search or have been actively looking for some time, you must stop and determine your value before moving forward. If you cannot convince potential employers you are the answer to their needs, you do not stand much of a chance of being hired.

You need to have a good understanding of your professional value before you can begin to broadcast it to others. If you don't know the value you can bring to an organization, you have no business interviewing with that organization. Period.

I cannot tell you how many job seekers I talk to who have no idea what they can do for an employer! They can recite all their experience, but they rarely can turn that into a clear statement of their value and why an employer would want to buy their skills. Telling me you want the job being advertised is not a compelling reason for me to hire you.

IF YOU CANNOT CONVINCE A POTENTIAL
EMPLOYER YOU ARE THE ANSWER TO THEIR NEEDS,
YOU DO NOT STAND MUCH OF A CHANCE OF
BEING HIRED!

So how do you determine your value?

To repeat, employers want employees to solve problems. So your value lies in how you can solve each potential employer's problems.

Your value comes from the blend of your SKILLS, EXPERIENCE, EXPERTISE, and STYLE. This is what you bring to the potential employer. Every tool you use, every strategy you implement, and every technique you incorporate in your job search must reflect your value.

Skills

Skills are the things you know how to do. Your skills are typically made up of soft skills and hard skills. Soft skills are personal attributes that enable you to interact effectively and harmoniously with other people. They are readily transferable, whereas hard skills are typically learned and may or may not transfer from one company to the next.

Soft skills are things like leadership, self-confidence, time management, problem solving, or having a positive attitude. These are skills that can be used virtually anywhere. They tend to be generic organizational and interpersonal skills. If you can supervise teams of office personnel or engineers, you're demonstrating soft skills that are easily transferable to a new employer.

YOUR VALUE
COMES FROM THE
BLEND OF YOUR
SKILLS, EXPERIENCE,
EXPERTISE, AND
STYLE.

Hard skills are usually the processes used by a specific industry or company. You may be an expert in ancient programming languages like FORTRAN for a small specialty company. But if the new job you are seeking does not involve programming, it is not a transferable skill. Similarly, you may know the building codes for Tulsa but not Los Angeles.

Experience versus Expertise

Your EXPERIENCE includes the accomplishments or highlights from time spent in a particular job and industry, whereas your EXPERTISE characterizes your specialized skill set. For example, two chemical engineers have the same experience of working at a major oil company for five years, but one has expertise in oil drilling while the other is an expert in refining. Lawyers may work for the same firm, but one may be an expert in contract law and the other in personal injury law.

So, experience is your past job **history**. It is where you have worked and the positions you have held. By comparison, expertise is the specialized **skill set** you carry with you that can be applied to new problems with new employers.

Style

Finally, your **style** is a reflection of your personality, your character, and how you interact with others. Your style will often impact your value to a company for a particular job.

For example, if an employer needs a salesperson who will make daily cold calls, he or she will likely want a gregarious people-person who is not discouraged by refusals. If you are a soloist who likes to sit alone at a computer terminal, then that sales position may not be the right job for you! You need to take your style into account on a job-by-job basis.

Right now, grab a piece of paper or sit at a computer, and make a list under each category of what you think are your strongest points in each of these categories. You MUST take the time to determine what value you really offer the business community at large, specific industry(s), and even potential specific employers.

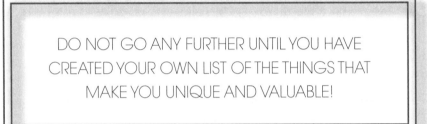

DO NOT GO ANY FURTHER UNTIL YOU HAVE CREATED YOUR OWN LIST OF THE THINGS THAT MAKE YOU UNIQUE AND VALUABLE!

Why You Stand Out From OTHER Job Seekers:

SKILLS:

_____

_____

_____

EXPERIENCE/Job History:

_____

_____

_____

EXPERTISE/Unique Special Skills:

_____

_____

_____

STYLE/Preferred Working Modes:

_____

_____

_____

CHAPTER TWO

YOU Are the Product and YOU Are the Salesperson

Once you've determined your value to the business community, you're ready to step into the role of marketer and salesperson.

Remember from the Introduction that there are **Four Milestones** to an effective product sale:

 PACKAGING—To clearly differentiate you from your competition (and the subject of this book).

 PROMOTION—So you are broadcasting your value, NOT your resume.

❸ PRODUCT DEMONSTRATION—Using innovative tools during the interview process to help you become the candidate of choice. Successfully answering critical interview questions is the secret to success in this milestone.

❹ PRICING—Where your true worth to the organization is measured by your total compensation package, not just salary.

The combination of these four milestones is designed to help you achieve differentiation. Differentiation is critical to ensure you stand out as the candidate of choice from the herd of other job applicants.

Another way of describing differentiation is branding or packaging.

Yes, I know you are not a tube of toothpaste or a fast-food chain. And I know it may be tempting to skip this step and go right to writing resumes and learning job interview techniques. But it doesn't matter whether you agree or like the idea.

Differentiation, branding, and packaging have become critical in successful job searches.

Tom Peters, in his 1997 *Fast Company* magazine article titled "The Brand Called You" (http://www.fastcompany.com/magazine/10/brandyou.html) said:

"We are CEOs of our own companies: Me Inc. Create a message and a strategy to promote the brand called You. ... You're every bit as much a brand as Nike, Coke, Pepsi, or the Body Shop. To start thinking like your own favorite brand manager, ask yourself the same question the brand managers at Nike, Coke, Pepsi, or the Body Shop ask themselves: What is it that my product or service does that makes it different?"

Don't get lost in the pile with everyone else's resumes and cover letters! Be seen as a solution to the company's problems and not another piece of paper!

Personal branding involves taking control of how you are perceived. So whether or not you like it or were aware of it, you already have a brand. Your brand is the combination of personal attributes, values, strengths, and passions that represent the value you offer. So it's up to you to identify those qualities and characteristics within you, bring all the pieces together, and communicate a crystal clear, consistent message that differentiates your unique promise of value and resonates with your target employer.

I do not know where you are in the process or familiarity with selling, but there are several good books on personal branding, including:

- *The Complete Idiot's Guide to Branding Yourself* by Sherry Beck Paprocki

- *Me 2.0, Revised and Updated Edition: 4 Steps to Building Your Future* by Dan Schawbel

- *Branding Yourself: How to Use Social Media to Invent or Reinvent Yourself* by Erik Deckers and Kyle Lacy (Que Biz-Tech)

- *You Are a Brand!: How Smart People Brand Themselves for Business Success* by Catherine Kaputa

- *Career Distinction: Stand Out by Building Your Brand* by William Arruda and Kirsten Dixson

YOUR MARKETING TOOLBOX

Building your package or brand takes tools. After analyzing what did and did not work in the Packaging milestone for job seekers, I discovered that there are **eight key tools** every job seeker should have in his or her toolbox.

TOOL NUMBER 1: YOUR 10-SECOND COMMERCIAL

Yup, just like toothpaste and fast food, you need a commercial to communicate your brand. You will use this commercial when meeting new people, networking, and in your interviews. You want to control the perception of others and that takes a 10-second commercial that allows you to communicate your value.

You want to give a positive, confident statement that explains your **expertise;** in other words, your specialized skill sets. I know it's hard to do that when you've been out of work for a while, but it's important to remember that you're still the same person with the same skills and expertise you had when you were employed.

When responding to the question "What do you do?" you don't want to respond with a statement like: "Well, I just got laid off and I'm looking for a job. Do you know anybody who is hiring?" This response is negative in its tone and almost always makes people feel uncomfortable. You also don't want to say, "Well, I was a sales manager before they laid me off." Again, a negative response. You should respond with something like, "I'm a senior sales manager looking to continue my career here in the local area. At the moment, I'm targeting some specific companies and industries to learn about potential opportunities."

There's a big difference between a positive and negative response. Let me give you a personal example. If someone were to say to me, "Nice to meet you Greg. What do you do?" I would respond, "I'm a Certified Career Management Professional. I enjoy teaching a strategic versus traditional approach to job search that helps my clients achieve differentiation and successfully compete in a very tough job market."

Too many people in transition fall into the habit of responding to the "What do you do?" question by saying "I **Was** …" instead of "I **Am** …" Your expertise is current! It didn't end when you left your last employer or transitioned out of the service. Remember, you're a professional first and someone else's employee second.

Be prepared to expand your 10-second USP commercial if asked to introduce yourself to a group. This often occurs in network meetings, and, in that setting, a longer introduction is expected and appropriate.

Note: You may have heard the term "elevator speech" or 90-second commercial. In my opinion you need to get sufficient information across in a much shorter period of time, especially when networking one-on-one. You want to be succinct and professional and talking too much or too long may be perceived as a negative by the other party. Just try talking for 90 seconds straight in the mirror. It feels like an eternity. Ten seconds is a snap and will allow you to maneuver into more strategic conversations.

TOOL NUMBER 2: PERSONAL BUSINESS CARDS

In Victorian England it was expected that people would carry calling cards, personal cards that included their contact information. These cards were presented when meeting someone for the first time, often delivered on a silver tray carried by the butler! This was considered good manners and provided a reference and memory tickler after the meeting/interview was concluded.

Guess what? What's old is new again! Using a personal card is so unique that it will leave an impression on everyone you contact in your job search!

Please note that we are not talking about a business card from your current or previous employer! This is a personal card that simply includes your name, designations (if any), personal contact information, and your functional expertise. For example, your personal card should have your name, telephone, e-mail, social media (if appropriate), and your area of expertise, such as operations management, logistics management, or supply chain management, etc. Including your home address is optional. The goal is to give the recipient a way to contact you so just telephone and e-mail may be sufficient.

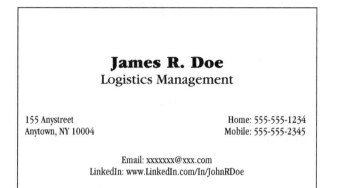

You don't need logos and fancy borders to make a good impression. Keep it simple and classic. White or ivory is best unless your industry expects wild and creative. Invest a few dollars and order cards that are on heavier stock.

Another alternative is business-card sized note cards from companies like http://www.Levenger.com. They come in both business card and 3 x 5 card sizes. You can use them like note cards for leaving messages or providing information to people you meet. WARNING: Don't use Internet providers of free business cards. While you may have a choice of designs, logos, etc., many people select the same format. These cards, in my opinion, generally look tacky and are unprofessional. Not only do they have the provider's name on the back of the business card, e.g., "free business cards at www.xyz.com," they may be flimsy and printed on cheap stock. This is not the impression you want to give. And don't print them on your home computer. Spend $50 and get 500 cards that look great. Staples, Office Max, and local print shops can assist you.

Your e-mail also has to be professional. WhosYourDaddy@vvvvv.com is not at all professional for job hunting. JohnJSmith@gmail.com or JaneJDoe@gmail.com is all you need. You may want to get a free Google Gmail account and attach the Google Voice option to it to ensure you don't miss calls!

TOOL NUMBER 3: RESUMES

Resumes and cover letters have been around since dinosaurs roamed the corporate earth. And like most traditions, they remain necessary components of your marketing toolbox.

You will need resumes and cover letters as part of your Packaging. However, DO NOT cling to the belief that your resume alone will get you in the door. The myth of the perfect or "killer" resume is just that, a myth. The truth is it's not happening like that in today's economy.

However, there are more effective tools to land a job than just a resume and cover letter. You'll read more about these tools that aid your job search success in the next section. But here we describe the necessary evil that is a resume.

Regardless of how professional your resume looks, how incredible your experience and accomplishments, how stunning your education, etc., your resume is just one of thousands and thousands and thousands. There is **no** differentiation—you just look like everyone else out there begging for a job.

Yes, I know that there is that rare individual whose resume hits the right desk at the right time and they get the dream job. I also hear about people winning the lottery or progressive slot machines for millions of dollars. But I wouldn't want to build my financial future on those rare examples and neither should you rely on just your resume winning the job lottery.

Regardless of the content, format, and presentation, your resume represents nothing more than a reflection of the past. Yet companies are interested in what you can do for them moving forward.

COMPANIES
DON'T HIRE YOU
FOR YOUR PAST;
THEY HIRE YOU
FOR THEIR
FUTURE.

Here's my definition of a resume:

> *"Resume (rez-uh-may): a necessary evil. A brief written account of professional qualifications, experience, accomplishments, and education that usually invites rejection from potential employers. Old-fashioned; generally lacking in effectiveness."*

Your biggest obstacle in using a resume as the lone tool for finding your next job is human resources. That's where a resume ends up. HR's job is to wrangle and strangle resumes. And that is assuming your perfectly crafted, beige, parchment paper resume gets past the new "meatgrinder" software it was scanned into and ends up in the hands of a real person! Virtually all companies with more than 25 employees now use meatgrinder software to eliminate candidates whose resumes lack the right keywords and longtail phrases.

The bottom line is that your resume does a lousy job of conveying your value to a potential employer. However, a professional resume is a tradition and is simply a necessary evil; therefore, yours must be a professional representation of your work experience, areas of expertise, accomplishments, and education.

There are three popular types of resumes: the chronological, combination, and functional resume. Included in the next chapter are samples of these resumes and explanations on how to create them. Use the examples as you create your own resume.

TOOL NUMBER 4: THE BIOGRAPHY

The biography is an essential component of your marketing toolbox and is an innovative tool that will clearly differentiate you from your competition. This unique tool is targeted specifically toward hiring managers in companies of interest and allows you to customize your approach by focusing on what you can do for that particular company moving forward.

Remember, your resume is nothing more than a reflection of the past and does a lousy job of conveying your potential value to an organization. Your biography will be the most effective tool you ever use in job hunting and will continue to be the best tool to differentiate you from the rest of the herd of commodity job seekers.

People often ask me what they should include in a biography. You're probably wondering the same thing. To be effective, your biography should be a brief, one-page summary of your professional background.

Let me suggest this scenario: Imagine that you're having a cup of coffee with a hiring manager who works for a company that you're interested in. This isn't an interview, it's a casual meeting. In the middle of the conversation, he or she asks "Tell me, how can you help our company?" You're not going to respond to this question by reciting your resume. Instead, you're going to present yourself in a conversational way, discussing how your skills, experience, accomplishments, and personal style could represent **added value** to this potential employer. What you say in this conversation becomes the foundation of your biography.

The biography is completely free-form, so you need to think about how you can best present what **you** offer to the marketplace in terms of your **value**. Typically, it should include a general summary of your experience and expertise, perhaps several soft skills, highlights or accomplishments (from any period in your career), and a generic forward-thinking statement—what you want to do next. In a biography, you don't have to mention names of the companies you worked for or even the industry you worked in.

There is no set format to the biography, so it can be all text, mostly bullets, or a combination of both. It's written in third person as if someone else is presenting you to the reader. For example, "Mr. Jones is an accomplished team builder ...," or "Ms. Smith earned her MBA..."

I prefer a shorter biography (using an opening paragraph, several bullets, and a closing paragraph), compared to a full page of text. But remember, it's your choice.

More information on the biography, along with a sample and associated cover letters, can be found in the following chapter. Be sure to look it over.

TOOL NUMBER 5: COVER LETTERS

Too many people use one standard letter. Whether using a traditional letter or strategic cover letters, make sure your cover letters are personalized to your targeted audience. Whether you're sending it to human resources, referral contacts, or a hiring manager, make sure you tailor it to that person. Be sure it gets your point across in a concise way that demonstrates self-confidence. Included in the next chapter are samples of these cover letters and explanations on how to create them. Use the examples as you create your own letter.

Traditional Resume Cover Letters

These particular letters begin by referring to the position you're applying for and its job code (if indicated). The meat of each letter demonstrates how your qualifications match the key job requirements, as listed in the ad. If the ad requests a salary history, give a range rather than a specific number. Unfortunately, whether you include or omit salary information, you still run the risk of being screened out.

End your letters with a closing statement expressing your eagerness to move forward to the interview process.

Strategic Cover Letters

Strategic cover letters are used to gather information as well as contact potential employers. These are usually requests for general information on the company or the industry. They are also used to request networking leads or contact someone to whom you were referred for additional information.

Most strategic cover letters here are **NOT** a request for a job interview or anything related to employment with that company! While you will include a biography or other general information, you will NOT include a resume. Resumes **scream** "I need a job" and you are **NOT** job hunting with the recipient. You **ARE** information hunting.

As with your resume, biography, and any other correspondence you may send, make sure your cover letters are accurate in terms of spelling and grammar.

Note: Included with TheHireRoad™ are numerous sample cover letters. These include traditional and strategic networking letters. Like other sample documents, they are in Word format, so you can easily customize them.

TOOL NUMBER 6: MANAGEMENT ENDORSEMENTS

We're all influenced by product endorsements that cause us to favor one particular product over another. In the context of a job search, the same is true for hiring decisions. Awards, letters of recommendation, certificates of achievement, and accolades extracted from your past performance reviews all endorse you as a candidate. These may strongly influence the hiring manager to select **you** over others.

Think about how you are influenced by testimonials and product reviews on websites and advertisements. Hiring managers are looking for similar validation and decision shortcuts! If other managers like you, you are less of a risk if hired. Think of management endorsements and awards as your equivalent of the Good Housekeeping Seal of Approval on your career.

Dig out past copies of your reviews and look for any statements made by former managers that are praiseworthy. Take four or five of those statements verbatim and list them on a single sheet of paper, in quotes. Be sure to identify the name, title, and company of the person who made the statement. You don't need to list a date.

Your management endorsements can reflect any period in your career. When reviewing performance reviews, look for those areas where you received a high mark or statements of praise that former managers have made concerning your performance. Make a note of these. Also make a list of any awards that you've received, such as employee of the month, year, etc.

Remember, you're entitled to copies of signed performance reviews, so if you can't locate your own copies, contact your former managers, and/or HR departments, and request them.

Take advantage of your management endorsements. You can paraphrase them in cover letters, resumes, and biographies, and you can take advantage of the actual wording of endorsements during the interview. You'll reinforce your value and provide additional reasons for the hiring manager to select **you** as the preferred solution.

If you are still on good terms with your previous employer and/or supervisors, you can ask them for current letters or e-mails. Don't be shy about asking for their help! Most managers are happy to assist within the restrictions of any rules and regulations.

Your management endorsements represent a fantastic tool to introduce during the all-important strategic interview and will clearly separate you from your competition. Samples of this tool, along with an explanation of the strategy, can be found in TheHireRoad™ job search tutorial.

TOOL NUMBER 7: THE POST-INTERVIEW PACKET

The post-interview packet is another innovative tool that should definitely be included in your marketing toolbox and will clearly put you head and shoulders above other candidates competing for the same job. Numerous clients have said that it was the post-interview packet that got them their job. It further differentiates you from the pack like the biography and management endorsements did on the front end.

This tool is sent directly to the hiring manager once the entire interview process is complete. While other candidates will be sending a typical thank-you letter, thank-you card, or an impersonal thank-you e-mail, you'll be providing a complete packet to the hiring manager that contains everything he or she needs to know to make the decision to hire YOU. The post-interview packet is generally made up of five sections:

1 Value Proposition (written in first person)

2 Biography and Resume

3 Management Endorsements

4 Education, Certifications, and Additional Training

5 References

Completed and sent overnight following the last interview in the process, the post-interview packet is designed to be sent directly to the manager who is making the decision to hire. If it's going to be a collaborative decision between several managers, send each a packet.

Your post-interview packet should be professionally presented in an inexpensive presentation folder, preferably with a clear cover. Use dividers or heavier card stock to label and separate each section.

Your target is the hiring manager, **NOT** human resources.

Hand-written thank-you cards should be sent to all others you met during the interview process. Personalize each of these cards by referring to something unique about each person you met. I would encourage you to avoid sending an e-mail thank-you. I believe they're impersonal and typically get lost in the myriad of e-mails that busy managers receive every day.

Your post-interview packet should include a cover letter that expresses your appreciation for the opportunity to interview, your interest in the company and the position, your reference to the enclosed interview packet, and your keen interest in entertaining an offer. End the letter with a statement that implies that, after receiving an offer, you look forward to being part of the organization and making an immediate contribution.

TOOL NUMBER 8: REFERENCES

Keep in mind that references are not the same as endorsements. References are generally used to validate employment in terms of title, length of employment, salary, and eligibility for rehire. Endorsements are awards, letters of recommendation, statements of praise, etc.

While you may already have an established list of references, it may change based on the discussion during the interview. For example, the hiring manager mentions a former manager of yours that he knows. If this former manager represents a good reference for you, you want to be sure to include his or her name on your list. Also keep in mind that a prospective employer may want additional contacts above and beyond your list, including one or two personal ones. Always follow their lead in providing the right type of references.

It's a good idea to maintain an up-to-date list reference list that you can use at any time. Be sure to notify those contacts before they receive a call from your potential employer and agree on the information to be provided.

ADDITIONAL MARKETING TOOLS

Sales Literature

Sales literature includes flyers or brochures that may be helpful if you're attempting to promote yourself as an independent consultant. If you're going to develop such tools, make sure they are professional in both content and appearance. This includes the correct grammar and no spelling errors.

Portfolio of Sample Work

This is a useful tool when applying for positions that involve creativity and design. For example, if you're applying for a marketing position, you want to present samples that display your writing, design, and creative talents. If you're applying for a web developer position, provide specific examples of websites. These could be either on CD or live.

CHAPTER THREE

Creating a Resume and Cover Letter

There are three typical resume formats: Chronological, Functional, and Combination:

THE CHRONOLOGICAL RESUME

The **Chronological** resume is most commonly used when your work experience reflects significant time, and perhaps advancement, with each employer. Such experience prepares you well for the type of job you're seeking. This format is also the most preferred by HR departments.

Note: Make sure you use the format preferred by each employer. Some will have specific requirements for submission. If in doubt, ask the HR personnel at each employer what they want from a job applicant. Simply asking can help differentiate you from the hundreds who don't!

THE FUNCTIONAL RESUME

If you're new to the job market, you're changing careers, or you have gaps in employment, the **Functional** resume will probably be a better choice. This format is typically used to highlight accomplishments that are broken down by function. Unlike the chronological resume, it doesn't focus on soft skills, employers, responsibilities, and dates of employment. Instead, your accomplishments and expertise are listed on the first page with your work experience listed in reverse chronological order on the second page, along with your education, certifications, etc. While you may be tempted to omit specific dates of employment, this omission may lead employers to think that you're withholding something.

THE COMBINATION RESUME

The **Combination** resume is a blend of both chronological and functional formats. With this format you're able to highlight those skills that are relevant to your current search by placing them in a special section by function to draw the reader's attention.

See examples of these resumes on the following pages.

SAMPLE CHRONOLOGICAL RESUME

YOUR NAME

Address   Cell: (555) 555-5555
City, State Zip   Email: yourname@xxxx.net

CHEMICAL ENGINEER

Accomplished professional offering significant experience and expertise in the area of thermoplastics manufacturing, including GPPS, ABS, HIPS, IRPS, & SAN. Strengths include technical knowledge, self-direction, prioritization, root-cause investigation, de-bottlenecking and process control programming. Demonstrated ability to impact profitability by effectively leading multi-functional teams and completing major projects on time. Able to consistently meet company objectives, many times with limited resources. Familiar with Six Sigma methodology and SAP. Core competencies include:

- Process Improvement
- Team Leadership
- Training & Development

- Analytical/Problem-Solving
- Mentoring
- Customer Service

PROFESSIONAL EXPERIENCE

CENTURY CHEMICAL COMPANY, Torrance, CA   1992 - 2005
Leading commodity & specialty chemical company with $33 BB annual revenue

SENIOR PRODUCTION ENGINEER (1999 - 2005)
Key technical resource for 3 production units. Responsibilities included troubleshooting production problems, operator mentorship, capital improvement facilitation, process control, plant maintenance coordination, operating procedure development and training program development. Provided backup support to quality coordinator, maintenance coordinator and production planner. Assisted Six Sigma project leaders in identifying opportunities, developing and implementing action plans, and measuring project success. Networked with other global production engineers to leverage learning experiences and standardize global operating procedures.

- Implemented the first standardized program for polystyrene production. The success of this project initiated a worldwide rollout of the program in 26 sites.
- Increased production efficiency by achieving a 20% reduction in transitional off-grade.
- Increased maximum asset output of two polystyrene production processes by 13.5%.
- Achieved a 7% increase in asset capability.
- Coordinated the scale-up of a successful pilot study to a full production process. The success of the production study helped launch the C-TECH® product line resulting in more than 1BB pounds in polystyrene sales.
- Collaborated with maintenance planner to safely complete over 12 shutdowns, identifying critical paths to minimize customer impact.
- Revamped IRPS compound extruder and retained $24MM in annual IRPS sales.
- Coordinated 12 shutdowns & start-ups without environmental or safety incident.
- Improved product consistency 20% by driving product properties to target.
- Identified and resolved intermittent catalytic reaction problem.
- Enhanced key customer relationship by identifying & removing contamination issue.

QUALITY COORDINATOR (1997 - 1999)
Managed plant quality program. Coordinated customer visits, investigated and resolved plant related customer complaints, maintained ISO, UL, and CSA certifications, participated in global production specification reviews, and maintained product physical property database.

- Mentored, identified priorities, and directed activities of lab technicians.
- Designed and executed experiments to improve product quality.
- Successfully resolved IRPS formulation issue, resulting in improved product performance throughout North America.

PROJECT MANUFACTURING REPRESENTATIVE - Midland, MI (1996)
Led project team through scope development, engineering, installation, and start-up. Guided project manager, process engineer, mechanical engineer, CAD designer, operations and programming support to ensure that the project was a success and met the needs of the plant.

- Successfully installed $1.5MM rubber dissolver and recycle tank resulting in a $2MM increase in project capacity.
- Led programming effort for feed system.
- Developed operating procedures and trained operators.

PRODUCTION ENGINEER - Midland, MI (1992 - 1996)
Provided technical support for 2 production units; troubleshot production problems. Identified and implemented production improvements, provided process control support, coordinated plant maintenance activities, created and updated operational procedures, calculated and reported annual air permit emissions.

- Improved plant capability by 40%.
- Led a multifunctional team to implement a new raw material that improved product quality and captured more business volume.

EDUCATION

South Dakota School of Mines and Technology
BS, Chemical Engineering (emphasis in polymers science)
Graduated Summa cum Laude

Typical traditional, same-old resume format

SAMPLE FUNCTIONAL RESUME

YOUR NAME

Address   Cell: (555) 555-5555
City, State Zip   Email: yourname@xxxx.net

MARKETING COMMUNICATIONS MANAGER

Creative, dynamic manager offering proven expertise in the successful development and execution of strategic integrated marketing activities. Significant experience in advertising, promotion, press relations, training programs and marketing campaigns Key competencies include:

- Messaging Consistency
- Editing
- Copywriting
- Training

- Written / Verbal Communication
- Public Relations
- Project Management
- Vendor Management

PROFESSIONAL ACCOMPLISHMENTS

MARKETING COMMUNICATIONS

- Achieved a 300% increase in sales while developing and effectively managing highly successful marketing campaigns and product launches.
- Recognized for increasing sales team awareness of company activities and national/international successes through the development of weekly newsletters, marketing bulletins, intranet website updates and quarterly video tapes.
- Co-developed and managed promotional marketing programs with channel partners.
- Developed self-paced manuals, sales presentations, competitive analyses and reference materials.

PROJECT MANAGEMENT

- Successfully developed and managed a corporate packaged services project and channel partner launch project which increased sales from initial $500,000 per month to $1.5 million dollars per month. Projects included package design, process development for warehousing, fulfillment, purchasing and registration, and nationwide training of corporate and channel partner sales force.

TRAINING

- Increased monthly sales from initial $500K to $1.5M through the effective training of channel partners and the sales team.
- Developed and organized new hire training programs for worldwide sales team.
- Interacted closely with internal departments which resulted in accurate and up-to-date training materials.
- Instrumental in the development of an award-winning "QuickStart" condensed training program that significantly reduced "time-to-market", and improved overall sales effectiveness.

SAMPLE FUNCTIONAL RESUME

YOUR NAME PAGE 2

PROFESSIONAL EXPERIENCE

SST TECHNICAL SOLUTIONS, Corona, CA   2002 - Present
MARKETING COMMUNICATIONS MANAGER

HEDLIND TECHNICAL SERVICES, Los Angeles, CA   1998 – 2002
SERVICE MARKETING MANAGER

PRINT-RITE, INC., Anaheim, CA   1994 – 1998
MARKETING PROGRAMS MANAGER

UNITED TECHNICAL, Brea, CA   1988 – 1994
WESTERN AREA TRAINING MANAGER (1989-1994)
SR. PRODUCT TRAINER (1988-1989)

EDUCATION

University of Oregon, Eugene, Oregon
B.S., Business Administration (Marketing)

YOUR NAME

Address   Cell: (555) 555-555
City, State Zip   Email: yourname@xxxx.net

INFORMATION TECHNOLOGY EXECUTIVE

Significant experience and expertise in the translation of business issues into business solutions through the effective implementation of Information Technology. Offering strong experience in project management with a focus on increased productivity, efficiency and cost reduction. Effective leader with the ability to build and motivate high performance teams. Exceptional communication and presentation skills with outstanding technical writing and presentation skills.

KEY AREAS OF EXPERTISE

- Emerging Technologies
- Business Development
- Strategic Planning
- Budget Management

- Training & Development
- Relationship Building
- Contract Negotiation
- Vendor Management

SELECTED ACCOMPLISHMENTS

- **Saved approximately $1.8 million** by implementing new software package that increased operational efficiencies in all three divisions.
- **Reduced costs by 27%** through the implementation of new PCs in conjunction with new host system.
- **Saved 22% telecomm costs since third quarter 2000** by reworking sub-standard contracts.
- **Assisted in securing a $1.3 million contract** by developing a system-wide program to access an external database.
- **Saved an estimated annual cost of $84,000** by overhauling antiquated EDI system.
- **Achieved a 24% increase in productivity** through the implementation of a company wide wireless two-way communication solution.
- **Enabled estimated $4.5 million revenues since first quarter 2000 while enhancing productivity** by evaluating and deploying Blackberry hand-held wireless two-way communication solution.

PROFESSIONAL EXPERIENCE

HHC WORLDWIDE, Santa Ana, CA   1998 – 2004
DIRECTOR, INFORMATION TECHNOLOGY

Directed staff of up to 12 IT professionals in five US locations. Determined assignments, workloads, and schedules of the IT team. Ensured effective Information Technology education, promotion, implementation, and communication throughout entire company. Recruited, hired, developed and mentored IT personnel. Managed cross-departmental training in office automation and information management tools.

SAMPLE COMBINATION RESUME

YOUR NAME   PAGE 2

QCB MANAGEMENT, INC., Los Angeles, CA   1995 – 1998
DIRECTOR, INFORMATION TECHNOLOGY

Planned and directed corporate IT department, creating all procedure definitions. Managed and allocated budget. Interviewed, selected, and hired IT staff. Implemented electronic document management system, controlling over 7,000 mission-critical data files on clients and providers. Brought frame-relay, and LAN/WAN computer technology to all thirteen remote locations. Provided Internet access, E-mail, and Intranet application accessible via WAN. Reported directly to president.

PREVIOUS EMPLOYMENT

WHITNEY AND & YOUNG LLP, Los Angeles, CA   1993 – 1995
SENIOR CONSULTANT

UNITY CORPORATION, Anaheim, CA   1987 – 1993
IT MANAGER

DATA CONCEPTS, INC., Cypress, CA   1984 – 1987
TECHNICAL CONSULTANT

EDUCATION

California State University, Fullerton, CA
BS, Computer Science

TECHNICAL SKILLS

- Software Development
- EDI (Electronic Data Interchange)
- Network & Systems Planning
- Windows XP/NT/9x

- MS Office, Visio, Project
- LAN/WAN Infrastructure
- Visual Basic, SQL
- Intranet, Extranet

There are hundreds of books and websites with suggested formats for resumes. Generally they will include the following:

Objective

While you may choose to have "Summary of Qualifications" or "Objective" at the top of your resume, remember you won't get more than a 15- to 30-second glance. HR is **not** going to take the time to read a summary paragraph to determine your specialized skills or expertise. I don't like objectives at the top of a resume. If it doesn't match that of the company with regard to the position you're applying for, you're rejected right away. They'll move right on to the next resume on the top of the stack. So therefore, in my opinion, replace "Summary of Qualifications" or "Objective" with your current title, the title you're seeking, or your expertise.

Area of Expertise

The very top should include your **NAME** and all **CONTACT** information. Below your contact information I would suggest you list, in bold, capital letters your area of **EXPERTISE**. This could be your title in your current or last position, the title you are seeking or your expertise in general. For example, you could have "Supply Chain Manager" as a title or "Supply Chain Management" as an area of expertise.

Three or Four Sentence Description of Experience

Listed below your expertise or title, you will want to provide three or four sentences describing your general experience and skills. As a rule of thumb, don't ever include anything on your resume that can be used as a reason to **not** hire you. For example, beginning your summary with "Over 35 years experience …" gives away your age immediately and can certainly work against you.

Skills

Listed below your description of skills and experience should be your key strengths or competencies. These are transferable or soft skills, represented by four to six bullet points.

Professional Experience

Listed below these soft skills is your professional experience, presented in chronological order beginning with your current or most recent employer. When you make a list of your years of experience, keep in mind that potential employers are only interested in what you've done over the last 12 to 15 years or so.

If you've had several positions with the same employer over a period of years, be sure to list the total number of years to the right of the employer name and location, and then the years in each position next to each title. Avoid listing the years for each position on the right side of the resume since it will create the impression of job-hopping, another reason to screen you out.

Note: You should only list years of employment, not months. If you list months, it can be detrimental to you in terms of creating the impression that you're a job-hopper. For example, if the length of employment was from November 2002 to January 2003, to the reader this indicates no more than three months of employment, which may lead to speculation as to the short tenure. However, this short term of employment could have been the result of circumstances beyond your control.

However, if you list 2002 to 2003, this could theoretically mean almost two full years of employment. The point is, if a hiring manager wants to know the specific time you spent with any employer, he or she will ask during the interview.

When you list each employer, indicate the type of business. Below that, list your most recent title and provide a one or two sentence description of your general responsibilities.

Accomplishments

In the context of your resume, accomplishments are things you've done that have benefited your employer. An easy way to state your accomplishments is to use the acronym P.A.R., which stands for problem, action, and results. For example:

Resolved customer service issues by creating new policies and procedures that resulted in a 40% decrease in customer complaints.

The "P," or problem, was the customer service issue; the "A," or action, was creating new policies and procedures, and the "R," or result, was a 40 percent decrease in customer complaints. Keeping your accomplishments up to P.A.R. is an easy way for you to explain how you have benefited your employer. When you list your accomplishments always try to begin each with an action verb.

When using P.A.R., you can list your problem, action, and results in any order, as long as you include all three elements. Let me give you an example:

Achieved a 40% reduction in customer complaints by implementing new policies and procedures which effectively addressed existing customer service issues.

For each employer, try to quantify your accomplishments using any type of numbers, such as percentages, dollars, quantities (doubled, tripled, etc.). Include one or two accomplishments for each year you worked for the company, listing them under the corresponding titles or positions you held. Try to make sure you have dollars signs ($), percentages (%) and other measurements in your resume if at all possible.

Education

If you've earned a college degree, indicate the name of the college, city and state, and degree earned. If you've earned several degrees, list the most advanced degree first. If you've attended some college, but did not earn a degree, be sure to list the college name, city, and state, and the focus of the course work. If you're a high school graduate and have not attended any college, list your high school and city and state. If you've attended college, even for any period of time, you need not include your high school education. If you have additional training, technical skills, and/or certifications, list these below the description of your education.

Personal Information

Do **NOT** list any personal information, such as marital status, number of children, hobbies or interests unless the information is pertinent to the specific opportunity. References, should **NOT** be listed on your resume. They should be presented at the appropriate time, which we'll discuss later.

MORE YOU SHOULD KNOW ABOUT RESUMES

There are a variety of things on your resume that could screen you out. It could be your name, which may indicate a certain ethnic origin and, therefore, potential difficulty with the English language. It could be your address, which may trigger relocation issues. It could be your former employers and how long you worked for them or how short a time you worked for them. It could be something that gives away your age. Other things that could screen you out could include your title, your experience, the industry you're in, your education, your lack of education, or even your affiliations.

Check for Errors

Make absolutely sure you check your resume for spelling and grammatical errors. Have several other people review it before submitting it to anyone. Don't rely on spell check when proofreading your resume. Remember, there are many words that can be used incorrectly that spell check will not pick up. For example, "principle software engineer" should read "principal software engineer." But since both "principle" and "principal" are valid words with different meanings, spell check will not catch that error. Just like hanger and hangar—one is something you put clothes on; the other is a place for aircraft.

There is absolutely no excuse for spelling and grammatical errors! Regardless of how professional, how impressive, and how accurate your resume is in terms of work history, it won't get you the job if it contains errors! While your resume may provide a number of potential reasons to screen you out, don't let sloppiness be the immediate cause for rejection.

Tell the Truth

A few words of advice: don't ever lie or stretch the truth on your resume. Research indicates that up to 50 percent of job seekers do just that, most commonly exaggerating their education. Creative writing is something that you often find in magazines and almost always in resumes. There are probably thousands of candidates out there who have been screened out because of their resume but who could have won the Pulitzer Prize for fiction!

Simple is Better!

Don't get creative in the appearance of your resume. I suggest that you don't use brightly colored paper, shading, boxes, pretty squiggly lines, or any kind of graphics. And don't include your picture, which is an unnecessary distraction. These are additional reasons to screen you out!

Additional Resume Tips

Stay away from resume distribution services. What these outfits do is take your money in return for bundling your resume with many others and sending them unsolicited to so-called inside contacts in companies all over the country. What do you think happens to the bundle of resumes received? You're right! They join the pile in the circular file. If you're approached by one of these resume distribution services, ask them for a sample list of their inside contacts. But don't hold your breath waiting for it!

With TheHireRoad™ job search tutorial, you have the ability to create a high-impact, professional resume. Included are a number of samples of each format along with a variety of suggested templates. They are all in Microsoft Word format, so they're easy to customize. The **Resource** section of TheHireRoad™ will allow you to view and customize resumes that best fit your needs.

For more information on resumes, and why they are a LOUSY tool for job hunting, see **SECTION 2** *Fire Your Resume!* in this book.

SAMPLE BIOGRAPHY

Following is the biography for a job seeker looking for a job in information technology. It is written in the third person and focuses on his accomplishments relative to both employment history and value to a similar/target employer.

Notice that it is much shorter than a traditional resume and is, in reality, a sales piece for the job seeker!

SAMPLE BIOGRAPHY
MANUFACTURING / OPERATIONS

YOUR NAME

Biography

Xxxxxxx Xxxx is a Senior Manufacturing/Operations Executive offering a proven track record in driving manufacturing and operations initiatives, and building partnerships with key business decision makers. He is well-versed in the nuances of world-class manufacturing operations, and has developed a reputation as a savvy businessman, strategic thinker, and "fire fighter". He is a skilled "hands-on" leader, trainer, and motivator with effective interpersonal skills at all organizational levels. He enthusiastically embraces challenges; immensely enjoys turning around troubled operations and seeing the results of his teams' collaborative efforts.

Mr. Xxxxx's areas of expertise include: 1) Operations Management; 2) Strategic Planning and Analysis 3) Business Process Optimization; 4) International Operations; and 5) Large Scale Project Management. Examples of his career accomplishments include:

- Consistently increased production output and reduced operating costs by utilizing World Class Manufacturing concepts (lean manufacturing, six sigma, theory of constraints, etc.) to rationalize manufacturing networks, minimize system complexity, and administer multi-site changes.
- Led Manufacturing Strategy team in the development of strategic manufacturing platform focused on supporting increasing current sales of $2 plus billion to $10 billion within ten years.
- Drove the operational plan and subsequent development of the annual production capability blueprint with vision of expanding current production capacity by 50% within three years.
- Served as Manufacturing Representative on multiple acquisition proposals, targeting companies with annual sales from $100 million to $3 billion. Assessed potential acquisition manufacturing and integration potential to conform to corporate visions.
- Directed activities to attain $40 million of cost improvements in company's procurement organization. Targeted implementation of projected $29 million of annual savings within first 6 months of tasking.

A creative and innovative thinker, Mr. Xxxxx has demonstrated throughout his career the ability to meet or exceed objectives, many times with limited resources. He takes great pride in his integrity, work ethic and professionalism. A results oriented strategic executive who can provide significant value in a fast paced environment, Mr. Xxxxx' s leadership style is to build consensus and commitment by valuing and empowering his team. He is a graduate of the United States Military Academy at West Point, New York with a Bachelor of Science in Applied Sciences and Engineering.

Mr. Xxxxx is looking to continue his career with a progressive company where his skills and experience in manufacturing operations can be fully utilized to increase revenue, improve the bottom line, and thereby contribute to the continued success of the organization.

Telephone: (555) 555-5555   E-mail: xxxxxxx@xxxxx.net

SAMPLE STRATEGIC VALUE LETTER

(for use with biography)

When you send a copy of your biography to a potential employer, you only have about ten seconds to make an impression on the recipient! So to help let the recipient know why you are contacting them and sending your biography, you need a short and clear cover letter.

Following is a format that has proven successful over the last twelve years with job seekers I have coached:

Date

Name
Title
Company Name
Address
City, State, Zip

Dear Mr. / Ms. Jones:

With over five years of experience in Xxxxxxxxx Xxxxxxxxxxx I am currently exploring opportunities within your industry, and your company is of interest to me. Please understand, I am *not* contacting you to ask for a job. My objective is to simply familiarize you with how my skills, experience and expertise could represent added value to you, and your organization, at some point in the future.

As a means of introduction I have taken the liberty of enclosing a brief one-page summary of my background that, as you can see, reflects significant experience in xxxxx, xxxxx xxxxxxxx and xxxxxxxxxxxx.

I understand your time is valuable, however, I would welcome the opportunity to introduce myself to you personally, perhaps sharing a cup of coffee or allowing me to buy you lunch. Please expect a call from me within the next several days to hopefully arrange a short meeting.

(OR)

Please expect a call from me within the next few days to hopefully chat for a few minutes and answer any questions you may have about my background.

Thank you in advance for your time and consideration.

Sincerely,

Your name

Enclosure

SAMPLE STRATEGIC JOB LISTING LETTER

(for use with biography)

Follow a dual approach when responding to a job listing (regardless of where you saw it). After sending a copy of your resume and standard cover letter to human resources (along with everyone else), differentiate yourself and significantly improve your odds by sending your biography (not your resume at this point) and this Strategic Job Listing Letter directly to the hiring manager/decision maker for that position. Your goal is to get to the person who actually knows what the job will entail and what skills and expertise are needed to help solve their problems! NOTE: Your biography is never sent to human resources.

Date

Name
Title
Company Name
Address
City, State, Zip

Dear Mr. / Ms. Jones:

I understand your organization is currently seeking a Marketing Communications Manager. With a strong background in both strategic marketing development and communications, within your industry, I am keenly interested in pursuing this opportunity with Xxxxxxx Xxxx, Inc.

As a means of introduction I have taken the liberty of enclosing a brief one-page summary of my background which, as you can see, reflects significant experience in all areas of marketing communications management -- including expertise in the support of product revenue growth through improved reach, branding and market share; expertise which has helped increase brand awareness and enhance the bottom line.

Please note that I have in fact forwarded my resume directly to your Human Resources department as requested in your job listing. However, I would be most interested in meeting with you directly to further discuss the value I can bring to your organization with respect to this position. Please expect a call from me within the next few days to hopefully arrange a convenient time for us to get together.

Thank you in advance for your time and consideration.

Sincerely,

Your name

Enclosure

STRATEGIC NETWORKING LETTER

(for use with biography)

Date

Name
Title
Company Name
Address
City, State, Zip

Dear Mr. / Ms. Jones:

Would you be interested in expanding your professional network? With an extensive background in the xxxxxxxx industry that's exactly what I'm attempting to do by writing to you with the clear understanding that I'm *not* asking you for a job.

Recognizing how quickly the rapid changes in business and technology can affect job stability for all of us, I'm sure you'll agree that the most effective way to minimize such uncertainty is to nurture a network of professionals who share similar experience and expertise.

As a means of introduction I have taken the liberty of enclosing a brief one-page summary of my background that, as you can see, reflects significant skills, experience and expertise in your industry.

I would welcome the opportunity to get together with you to discuss how we can be of mutual benefit in maintaining the value we both represent to the business community. Please expect a call from me within the next few days to arrange a short meeting at your convenience.

Sincerely,

Your name

Enclosure

STRATEGIC MEETING LETTER

(for use with biography)

Date

Name
Title
Company Name
Address
City, State, Zip

Dear Mr. / Ms. Jones:

I am contacting you to ask for your help. With an extensive background in Xxxxxxxxx and Xxxxxxxxxx I am currently exploring opportunities within your industry and I'm gathering information from a variety of sources. I'm particularly interested in your views and perspectives with regard to some of the key challenges for companies in the industry and your advice as to where my skills and experience may best be utilized.

As a means of introduction I have taken the liberty of enclosing a brief, one-page summary of my background that, as you can see, reflects significant expertise in all areas of xxxxxxxxxxxxx, xxxxxxxxx, xxxxxxxxxxxxxxxxx, and xxxxxxx.

Recognizing the value of your time I would welcome the opportunity to spend a few minutes with you, perhaps sharing a cup of coffee or allowing me to buy you lunch. I'd also like to learn about your background since, while I'm actively networking within the industry, there may be an opportunity to assist you in some way. Please expect a call from me within the next few days to hopefully arrange a short meeting at your convenience.

Thank you in advance for your time and consideration.

Sincerely,

Your name

Enclosure

STRATEGIC REFERRAL LETTER

(for use with biography)

Date

Name
Title
Company Name
Address
City, State, Zip

Dear Mr. / Ms. Jones:

I am contacting you to ask for your help. With a strong background in Product Management I am currently exploring opportunities within your industry, and I'm hoping that you may be able to suggest one or two individuals I could talk with to get further information.

As a means of introduction I have taken the liberty of enclosing a brief one-page summary of my background which, as you can see, reflects significant experience and expertise in all areas of Product Management, expertise which has helped increase brand awareness and enhance the bottom line.

I will call you within the next few days to hopefully chat for a few minutes and get the name of one or two people I could contact.

Thank you in advance for your time and consideration.

Sincerely,

Your name

Enclosure

STRATEGIC RESEARCH LETTER

(for use with biography)

Date

Name
Title
Company Name
Address
City, State, Zip

Dear Mr. / Ms. Jones:

With an extensive background in xxxxxxxx xxxxxxxxxxxx I am currently exploring new opportunities in your industry. As a result of this research I have concluded that your company, its products and its culture represent a good match for my qualifications and interests. My research has also indicated that your company may currently be facing one or more of the following challenges:

- Xxxxxxx xxxxxxxx xxx xxxxxxxxxx xxxxx, xxxxxxxxxxxx, xxx xxxxxxxx.
- Xxxxx xxxxxx xxx xxxxxxxx xx xxxxxxxxx
- Xxxxxxx xx xxxxxxxxx xxx xxxxx xxxxx, xxxxxxxx xxx xxxxxx

As a means of introduction, I have taken the liberty of enclosing a brief summary of my background which reflects significant experience and expertise in all areas of xxxxxxxx xxxxxxxxxxxxx. Such expertise would be a great asset in helping to address the challenges that I have listed, in addition to others you may be facing with respect to their impact on your bottom line.

I would welcome the opportunity to discuss in greater detail how I can bring value to your organization. Please expect a call from me within the next few days to hopefully arrange a short meeting.

Thank you in advance for your time and consideration.

Sincerely,

Your name

Enclosure

SUMMARY

Differentiation is going to be the key to your successful job search. And the first step in setting yourself apart from others is to develop the tools that you'll need to market yourself effectively. The strategic tools I've talked about in **Packaging You!** are dynamic and designed to help you achieve your key objective of standing out to be outstanding.

Now that your marketing toolbox is completed, with both traditional and innovative tools, you're ready to move on to the second milestone down TheHireRoad™ which is **Promotion**. Here's where you have a distinct choice:

Option 1: Do I fall victim to the traditional approach to finding employment by relying on my resume to get me in the door, or

Option 2: Do I decide to educate the business community by broadcasting my value, NOT my resume?

If you're tired of the C.R.A.P. approach to job search you'll choose Option 2.

You MUST learn how to broadcast your value and achieve differentiation. That is the focus of *Fire Your Resume!*, which provides compelling reasons to avoid the resume shotgun and C.R.A.P. approach. You'll learn the seven specific tactics for a successful job search and receive samples of associated cover letters to accompany your biography.

However, there are more effective tools to land a job than just a resume and cover letter. You'll read more about these tools that will aid in your job search success in the next section.

SECTION 2

Fire Your Resume!

CHAPTER FOUR

The "Traditional" Job Search Approach

Competing in today's job market is incredibly stressful. And it doesn't help when the supposedly tried and true methods just aren't working. But everyone keeps using them!

Despite being shown this fact every day, recruiters (and virtually all books on the subject) still tell you that all you need to get in the door is a great resume.

If you're a typical job seeker you keep yourself busy by sending out hundreds of resumes in response to posted jobs found in the newspaper, on company websites, on Internet *job boards,* and anywhere else you can find them. Then you sit back and wonder why the phone's not ringing. Even though your resume screams that you are a perfect fit for that perfect job, you don't get a response. Maybe you were contacted by a "headhunter" or professional recruiter and it went nowhere.

Your job hunt is probably giving you one heck of a headache, right? It's probably taking a toll on your personal relationships and your self-esteem. It's hard work sending out all those resumes. I know, because I did it myself years ago when I was in transition and I talk to hundreds of job seekers every month who are doing exactly the same thing.

In your frustration, maybe you're considering a resume distribution service because of their "targeted approach" or their "direct access to hiring managers." Some of these services tell you that your resume will "reach thousands of recruiters in your industry" or that their program "allows recruiters and Human Resources (HR) managers to contact you instantly."

Do you really think your resume is going to get noticed among the thousands of others these services bundle together and practically spam to HR professionals nationwide? Yeah, I didn't think you did.

DON'T WASTE YOUR MONEY!

Who really posts on job boards?

The **#1 dirty little secret of job hunting** is that the majority of these resume bundlers—job boards and want ads in places like Craigslist and the local newspaper—are really in the business of resume preparation, interview training, and other "services" for job seekers. They are **not** really in the business of finding you a job! After all, the job board is free so where are they making their money?

When they blast your resume out to "thousands of companies looking for your qualifications," you will get very few (if any) serious responses. That predictable lack of response gives the bundler or board owners a reason to tell you that your resume is the problem! Then they try to upsell their "professional" resume-writing services, job-search training, or their "special limited-time-only gold package" and who knows what else to make a buck off your desperation and frustration.

Oh, and don't be surprised if the responses you do get all come from companies looking to train you to sell life insurance, do network marketing, work at home, attend an online school, go to a trade school, or sign-up for webinars for all manner of "opportunities."

The time you spend posting to job boards is basically wasted. The boards are more interested in selling you stuff than finding you a job!

Also, all the different job boards often simply scrape the same information from all the same sites. We have seen the same job listed on four or five different job boards as "exclusive." They often link to key employers in an area and many simply pull up the want ads from newspapers in the geographic area you specify! We have clicked on a job for a client and had it link to three different sites (planting Internet cookies each time it linked) before coming to rest on an employer site.

But what about career lists on the company websites? Aren't they legitimate?

Career pages on a company website are generally more legitimate than job boards. But they are usually the same listing you will see on the job boards. Also, the bigger the company, the more likely they are to use a computer program to assess your uploaded resume, which could eliminate it before a human being ever sees it!

To put it bluntly, your resume is doing a lousy job, so:

FIRE IT!

Note: I don't want you to think you don't need a resume at all. When I talk about resumes, I am talking about using them as your response to a job listing or as your door opener. As a tool for the first contact, it is no longer a success tool!

That said, resumes are STILL a "necessary evil." You must have one when asked for it. And just like a business card, you WILL be asked to present your resume at some point in the job-search process. Therefore, make sure it is free of typos, bad grammar, slang, etc. Make it keyword rich and a perfect fit to the organization.

"If you have not prepared a resume for some time, have gaps in employment, or are not confident in your ability to present yourself in the right way, I would strongly encourage you to consider the services of a professional resume writer. These individuals can provide you with a polished, professional resume that is free of errors and clearly displays your most important and compelling information."

A resume needs to be a professional representation of your work experience, accomplishments, and education. However, while yours may reflect solid work experience and past performance, it does little to convey the true value you bring to a particular organization moving forward. It is no longer the way to start the hiring process.

CHAPTER FIVE

Four Reasons Not to Send a Resume

The "HR black hole" is a common term used in the recruiting world that refers to the futility of sending your resume through normal channels like human resources or other internal hiring departments.

Clever job seekers think they can get noticed by sending their resume directly to hiring managers (potential bosses who ultimately make the decision to hire). However, 99 percent of the time those resumes will **also** end up back in a pipeline to the HR black hole. Here are four reasons not to send a resume.

REASON 1—RESUMES END UP IN HUMAN RESOURCES

When you send a resume in response to a job listing, odds are your resume will end up in a stack a foot high, or in a database of thousands, and will be viewed for no more than 15 to 30 seconds. In addition, your resume will be seen by someone in HR personnel—not by the hiring manager. HR does not make the hiring decision unless you're applying for a position in the personnel department.

Do you really want personnel deciding if you're valuable enough to put in front of the hiring manager for an interview, or do you want the hiring manager making that decision? Most job seekers I know want the hiring manager making that decision!

Even so, because you're a job seeker who's attempting to change careers, your resume will now actually be working against you. It will scream to HR staffers, "I'm changing careers" and that is **not** a good thing when you are looking for a job.

REASON 2—RESUMES ARE USED TO SCREEN YOU OUT

HR departments are inundated with resumes, so they are using today's scanning technology more and more as a filtering tool. This is especially true if you upload your resume online. But if you send in a paper resume, they will literally scan it into their system so they can run it through a software program that looks for keywords matching the job description.

While you may have solid qualifications, your resume can present many reasons to reject you, including lack of keywords and/or phrases, job history, gaps in employment, affiliations, education, and current location, among others. Conversely, you may have negative keywords and dates that may be used to eliminate you. The whole HR process starts with rejection. They just don't want to hire anyone new unless they absolutely must.

When companies have decided they must hire someone, they start by looking for a mythical person fitting a perfect description. While the job description they write is basically a wish-list, your resume must match up to as many keywords and phrases as possible in order to be moved to the short stack of applicants.

You have been told over and over again that the best approach to get noticed and avoid rejection is to write directly to the hiring manager of a company, enclosing your powerful resume along with the best cover letter you've ever written.

The harsh reality is that as soon as your resume is pulled from the envelope it makes several statements loud and clear:

"I'm out of work (or will be) …"

"I'm looking for any job…,"

"I'm not happy with this position/employer/industry..."

"I need more money …"

"Are you doing any hiring…?"

With those ugly phrases ringing in the hiring manager's head, what does he do with your resume? It's either tossed into the trash or, most likely, forwarded to human resources where it stands an excellent chance—more than 95%—of being summarily rejected.

If you're lucky, you may get a courtesy "no thanks" letter or e-mail. But most of the time—you sit, waiting for the phone call that never comes.

REASON 3—RESUMES ARE NOT VALUE PROPOSITIONS

Resumes, though still used today, have a format that doesn't allow you to showcase your true talents. The resume's restrictive structure is merely a validation of what you've done in the past; it does **not** represent what you can do for a specific targeted company in their future.

Your value is much more than your education, training, and track record of employment and career accomplishments that were beneficial to any former employer(s). Hiring managers are not mind readers; therefore they cannot interpret information about you that doesn't appear on your resume.

When an employer decides to invest time and money to acquire your talent, they're not interested in what you've done in the past but what you can do for them now. It's all about the value you bring to the table: your ability to address the problems and challenges the company is facing that will increase profitability.

One of the rules of thumb for a successful written communication with a potential employer is to check it for symbols like dollar signs ($), percentages (%), and other direct measurements. If you don't see a liberal sprinkling of $, %, and # in your resume and other communications, go back and rethink what you did.

Hiring managers also know that resumes are an exercise in creative writing. Many job seekers stretch the truth or outright lie on their resume in an effort to get noticed. While you may not be lying or stretching the truth, your resume is a poor representation of who you really are because its format only allows you to present your employment history and education, nothing more. You need to convey your value, and tell them what is in it for **them** and their company to hire you!

Even powerful resumes, whether chronological, functional, or combination, have the same structure for writing and presentation of content. Even when embellished with accomplishments, decorations, and jargon, they probably don't include the elements of "fit"—which is the most important factor in a hiring manager's decision to hire.

REASON 4—RESUMES DO NOT DIFFERENTIATE YOU

Your biggest challenge in job searching is differentiation. In other words, how do you separate yourself from everyone else in a fiercely competitive job market? Are you sure your resume makes you stand out from the crowd? Do you think listing your awards and decorations will help?

Think again. All resumes look the same, including yours.

We are absolutely sure you are using one of the classic formats for resumes that everyone is taught to follow. You're required to list your name, contact information, education, experience, references, and awards. The format hasn't changed since the 1950s.

Same old, same old.

Do you really think you'll get noticed waving your resume in the air, begging for a job among the hundreds of thousands, if not millions, of other job seekers using the same pricey linen paper in an elegant color?

Maybe you've tweaked your resume day after day, week after week, and now you probably think your resume is one in a million. Well guess what? It is—just one of millions! It's another piece of paper, another entry into the database. It is nothing unique.

No matter how professional it looks, no matter how impressive your experience, how amazing your accomplishments, or how stunning your education, your resume is a resume.

Regardless of its format, your resume looks like everyone else's resume. Therefore **you** look like everyone else, too. Using a resume is not the way to stand out from other resume providers.

CHAPTER SIX

It's Time to Change Your Mindset!

The traditional approach to job searching, which involves spending countless hours sending hundreds of resumes in response to job postings found through Internet job boards, company websites, newspapers, trade publications, the unemployment office, or wherever they can be found, is **reactive**.

That means you are hunting and waiting for something to pop up in your line of sight. You are waiting for your "go" button to be pushed.

Being reactive can be ineffective. You are waiting for someone to hit the enter key and post a job so you can leap into action and send a resume.

You feel helpless because you are.

You are not in control.

You are waiting for the other side to make a move. And waiting for the other guy to make a move is a bad tactic for job hunting.

If you're following the traditional approach then you are waiting to get noticed. You're waiting for someone to pick your resume out of the stack. You are waiting to be seen as better than the rest.

You're waiting for something to happen.

And I know from experience that for all your hard work, the response has predictably been dismal. How many responses have you gotten for your efforts? 1 out of 20 resumes? 1 out of 50? More likely, 1 out of 100!

If you are LUCKY, an autoresponder e-mail will acknowledge your submission. Then, if you are VERY lucky, you might get a "no thanks, we are pursuing other avenues" e-mail. Forget a call or letter.

Why?

Because the odds are stacked against you, big time.

STOP WORRYING ABOUT FINDING A "JOB," AND START THINKING ABOUT YOUR EMPLOYABILITY!

You need to become **proactive**. You need to stop waiting for the call and make the call. You need to be the one pursued not the other way around.

You need to change your mindset and learn better tactics.

And better tactics start with better information.

Believe it or not, advertised jobs only represent less than 25 percent of all open positions out there. Publically posted jobs represent just the tip of the iceberg. The other 75 percent or so are below the surface in what's called the hidden job market.

We don't know about these jobs because they're not advertised. Yet these jobs are opened and filled every day.

The reason for this proportion is reflected by the way companies hire. If a company has a critical position they need to fill, they have four resources to find the best candidate. In order of preference they are:

RESOURCE 1—INTERNAL CANDIDATES

This is an employer's best choice. This is literally posting the openings on a bulletin board or through company mail. However, filling internally is not always practical. Promoting someone from within usually creates another void that needs to be filled. This is especially true in smaller companies.

Tactical Idea 1: Look for smaller companies that announce promotions in the local press. When someone is promoted there is often a position they previously held available.

Tactical Idea 2: Look for announcements of new contracts, new construction, and/or new projects at companies in the local news. These are potential opportunities for jobs!

RESOURCE 2—REFERRAL/ RECOMMENDATIONS/WORD-OF-MOUTH

This is the second-best choice. Sometimes employers will even offer bonuses to employees who recommend someone who is subsequently hired as a result of that referral. If no internal recommendations are made, the employer has two remaining options—both undesirable, but evil necessities in business—post the job and hire a recruiter.

RESOURCE 3—POSTING A JOB OPENING

This is not what a company wants to do. Posting a job triggers an avalanche of paper and e-mails into HR. Not only does this create resume overload, it can often cause the strongest candidates to be overlooked. This is not the optimum way to find the best employees.

RESOURCE 4—HIRE A RECRUITER

If a mountain of resumes has failed to yield the right candidate for the position, this leads to yet another undesirable choice for the employer. Hefty fees need to be paid to headhunters to find the right candidate. However, the more exclusive the job the more likely a recruiter is to be involved. The higher the pay, the more likely a company is to want a third-party to find and filter candidates.

Most companies fill 75 percent of their jobs through referral, recommendation, and word-of-mouth (Resource 2). Therefore, the majority of the time it's not necessary to publicly post a job opening where the general job hunting public can see it. But did you know that companies will still post jobs they already have candidates for?

The **#2 dirty little secret of job hunting** is that even though a position has been filled, companies will still post the job opening in order to comply with various hiring regulations and government policies. They may need to show community or minority outreach. If a hired candidate is a foreign national, they may need to prove to immigration that there are no American candidates equally qualified so they need tons of unqualified resumes as proof. And to ensure the widest possible visibility for the job proof, companies will use the big job boards as well as their own career pages.

Yet 99 percent of job seekers choose to focus on the 25 percent tip of the iceberg—the openly advertised jobs.

Why? Because it's easy!

How hard is it to wake up on a Monday morning, make a cup of coffee, stagger over to the computer in your bathrobe, and start to scroll down job after job after job on Internet job boards and company websites? Not very hard and, therefore, not very productive!

Relying on Internet job boards is a very frustrating and unproductive exercise. You need to realize the fierce amount of competition you face for each and every one of these posted jobs you apply for. Regardless of your qualifications, your odds of getting noticed are very slim to none.

So how do you improve your odds?

You start with better strategy, superior tactics, and a change of focus.

Better strategy: While your competition will be following the traditional C.R.A.P. approach to finding a job, you're going to implement a strategic approach that will focus on differentiation. Your success will result from your ability to clearly separate yourself from all others in today's highly competitive job market.

Superior tactics: Instead of spending all your time playing the Internet Lottery, you'll be educating the business community about who you are and the value you bring to the table. As you develop your professional network and start to connect with hiring managers, you'll be employing innovative tools, including your biography, strategic cover letters, management endorsements, and post-interview packet. These tools will not be used by your competition.

You start with **better strategy** and **superior tactics.**

You **change your focus** from getting a job to securing an interview.

You **change your focus** from getting your resume noticed in a pile of paper or e-mails to getting in front of the people who can see that you are more than a chronological resume.

You **change your focus** to acquire multiple targets of opportunity.

CHAPTER SEVEN

Tactics for a Successful Job Search in the New Economy

You've already completed the first tactic to finding a job: You fired your resume!

TACTIC #2—TARGET COMPANIES, NOT JOBS

This is the **big** shift you need to make in your thinking! Decide what geographical areas you'd like to work in and how far you're willing to commute to get to a job. Will you move? How big a company must it be? How much traveling? What kind of work environment—laid-back or button-down? Action oriented or steady? Nine-to-five or flexible, long hours? Rigid chain of command (like the police) or loose teams? What are the opportunities for advancement, benefits, etc.?

Determine all the critical factors for your life when you get a job. How flexible are you? What is important, what is "nice" versus a non-negotiable must-have? What can you compromise on? What is a deal breaker?

Then begin to research real companies of interest to you within that defined scope. At this point, as you go through this exercise, you don't care whether your targeted companies are hiring, firing, upsizing, sidewinding, or downsizing. Your goal is to find out more about the companies that fit your criteria. Whether they have jobs comes later.

All you know is that you'd like to go to work for any one of these companies sooner than later and if you were able to work for any one of them, you would bring added value. In other words, they could use your skills, experience, and expertise.

It's not very effective to simply respond to job postings online and wait for a call. It only makes you one of dozens (if you are lucky) but most likely hundreds who are doing the same thing with each of those postings. It is much more effective to pick one, or five, or ten companies you most want to work for, and execute a strategy to target them whether they have an appropriate opening posted or not.

Create your target list. Start by searching people on LinkedIn in your area with titles similar to what you are looking for. What companies do they work for? Pick the ones who match your experience and criteria best. (See Chapter 8 if you are unfamiliar with LinkedIn.)

Search LinkedIn and ask in other networks (Chambers, trade associations, Meetup, BNI, etc.) for contacts at those companies. Create your list of phone numbers and e-mail addresses for each one. You can use WhitePages.com, Jigsaw, and Google to help. Often by Googling the person's name you can find a direct phone number or e-mail address, or at least find the general format for the company e-mail addresses, then apply it to the individual's name. At the very least, you can certainly find the company's main phone number to call and ask for the person by name.

Learn what you can about those companies. Read their websites, Google them. Search for local news and announcements. Check finance sites for news about them. Check what kind of jobs they may have posted. Figure out what skills, experience, knowledge, and strengths you have that may uniquely fit their organization. **Hint:** Use the news section of the local paper or search online to see what new projects, contracts, or issues they may have that you can help solve for them.

If you're like most job seekers, you've heard about the importance of networking. So right now be prepared to spend about 15 percent or so of your time expanding your network by connecting with various people through real-world groups and social media. You are building a team to help you succeed in your mission!

Warning: As you start to network with people in your job hunt, you will soon find that some of your social contacts are looking to sell services, are other unemployed people, or are multi-level/network marketing associates. You will attend events where you may find yourself surrounded by those folks "desperate for a sale" socializing with the "desperate for a job" folks.

Using what you've learned, create a tailored set of qualifications and keywords to emphasize your strengths for each organization. Write them out.

TACTIC #3—DEFINE YOUR VALUE

Now that you've identified specific companies of interest, the next step is to determine your value to each of those companies. Take what you learned in Tactic #2 and describe your skills, experience, knowledge, and strengths that may uniquely fit their organization or solve a problem for them. Write them out. You will be using them for letters, your resume, interviews, networking, etc., with anyone in that company or industry.

Remember what we said earlier: companies don't hire you for your past; they hire you for your future—more precisely **their** future. While a strong resume and track record may be a good indicator of future performance, it does little to effectively convey the value you offer moving forward to a particular organization.

As mentioned in Chapter One, **value** is a blend of your **skills, experience, expertise,** and **style.** Let's take a look at each of these four components:

Skills

Your skills include both hard and soft skills.

Hard skills are typically learned skills. For example, we're not born with the ability to create an Excel spreadsheet; that's something we need to learn, just like driving a forklift, operating a lathe, or cooking. Hard skills typically refer to technical or administrative skills related to a company's core business.

That means hard skills may or may not transfer from one company to the next. Let's say you've been working as a certified forklift driver. You now want to go to work processing loan applications for a mortgage company in the financial services industry. In this case, your skill as a forklift driver does not transfer to the mortgage company because it's not relevant to the loan processing position. However, at this stage, list **all your skills.** You will pick and choose them later depending on the needs of the target employer!

Soft skills on the other hand are almost always transferable. These skills are referred to as behavioral competencies and are often described as "people skills" or "interpersonal skills." These skills are simply how you communicate with others—be it your clients, family, or friends—and they are crucial for success, especially in your career and business life.

Key interpersonal skills include communication, assertiveness, conflict resolution, and anger management. Good communication skills require that we listen as well as speak. We need to understand others, not just be understood ourselves.

Assertiveness skills enable us to express ourselves clearly without infringing on the rights of others. Conflict is all around us all the time, so it's essential to be able to resolve differences with others in order to maintain relationships that are important to us. Finally, anger management skills allow us to vent our annoyance in an appropriate, healthy way when dealing with emergencies and solving problems that confront us on a regular basis.

Experience

In defining the value you offer a potential employer, your experience should be generally stated—generically, without reference to your former employers, dates of employment, etc. Your experience is a key ingredient to the success you've had in previous jobs and a key element in being successful in a future job.

Experience gives you a feeling of personal growth and earns respect from others. Your career to date has been a continuous chain of experiences that have not only helped you learn, but have contributed to the value you offer the business community and a future employer.

Expertise

Your expertise refers to your *specialized* skill-sets, your skillfulness by virtue of possessing special knowledge. For example, being an environmental engineer is a skill, being an oilfield environmental engineer with knowledge of storm water pollution prevention plans (SWPPP) is expertise. Being an Internet social media expert is a skill; knowing how to program a Facebook iFrame Page is expertise.

Can you provide innovative solutions to your customers, whether internal or external? Do you thoroughly understand the products and services of your company and, more important, how they meet the needs of the customer? Do you add value to your company by coming up with new solutions to problems and issues related to your job?

While you may have a wide range of functional skills that you have developed over the course of your career, you may well have special or unique *expertise* in several areas.

Style

Your style is all about you as a person. It's what makes you unique.

It is also how you carry yourself in terms of your sense of manners, decorum, and values. It's a blend of your personality and character traits such as your dependability, honesty, integrity, compassion, enthusiasm, and faith in others that make you a desirable employee for most companies—once they know how you can help them achieve their goals!

Your style is also a reflection of your attributes, such as your resourcefulness, imagination, energy, initiative, insightfulness, motivation, and intelligence. It's also how you're perceived by your peers and your superiors.

If you don't know how a company rolls—ask current employees. Ask the local vendors. Do your research. This is important. If you are not a gregarious joiner, a job in a firm that promotes rock-and-roll events at casinos or bars is probably not a good fit. If you want to leave the regimentation behind and go back to your surfer days, a job as a police officer may not be a good choice.

TACTIC #4—TARGET THE HIRING MANAGER

Keep in mind that sending your resume into targeted companies where you'd like to go to work and where you know you would bring added value is not enough.

You need to identify the hiring manager in each of those companies. In other words, you need to identify the person who would be your potential boss. That's the one person in the organization who can truly appreciate the value you bring to the table.

How do you find the names of hiring managers in your targeted companies? This is where your professional network comes in, particularly the people you're connected with on the business-oriented social media site LinkedIn. (If you're not already on LinkedIn you need to be! It's free, and it's a fabulous tool to help you not only build and nurture a professional network, but also to gain exposure to the business community and identify targeted hiring managers.)

TACTIC #5—GET REFERRED TO THE HIRING MANAGER

Without a doubt, the best way to get an interview is to be referred to the hiring manager by someone he or she trusts.

Again, this is where LinkedIn can help. Use LinkedIn to research your targeted company to find out who's working there now and who has worked there in the past. Then use your network of professionals to connect with current or former employees of your targeted company and ask for their help in identifying the hiring manager. Finally, ask your connection if you can use their name when corresponding to the hiring manager. This is what's called a warm referral.

There is also a great book called *Selling to VITO: The Very Important Top Officer* that outlines ways of getting to the decision-makers in a company. The techniques outlined in the book are real-world calls, letters, and e-mails that still are powerful tools for job seekers!

TACTIC #6—BROADCAST YOUR VALUE, NOT YOUR RESUME

I am a big fan of educating the business community about who you are, and the potential value you can offer. But educate **without** using your resume as an initial means of introduction.

Now that you've defined your value in general terms, you need to convey that value to your targeted hiring managers. How?

This is where your **biography** comes into play.

In the context of job-search strategy, your biography is designed to pique the interest of the reader. Customized to address a specific company and hiring manager, it's a critical component of your marketing toolbox.

Let's take a closer look at the typical characteristics of your new job-hunting biography.

— One-page summary with no set format.

— Written in third-person. For example:
   Ms. Jones has extensive expertise in…
   She implemented a process improvement program that…
   With training in medical logistics, Ms. Jones…

She has significant experience with...
Ms. Jones adds value through her unique ability to...

— Free-form with respect to content. You can include, or exclude, whatever you want.

— Refers to key competencies/transferable skills. For example:
Mr. Johnson's areas of expertise include: operations management, strategic planning and analysis, business process optimization, international operations, and large-scale project management.

— Highlights accomplishments in a generic way. For example:
Led transition of distribution and service facilities, resulting in an annual expense reduction of more than $1M.
Received "Innovator of the Year" award for 2003 and 2004.

— May or may not include references to educational background.

— Concludes with future aspirations; a forward-thinking statement of what you want to do for that company, job, or industry. For example:
Mr. Johnson is looking to continue his career with a progressive company where his significant skills, experience, and expertise in manufacturing operations can be fully utilized to increase revenue, improve the bottom line, and thereby contribute to the continued success of the organization.

Remember that your value is best conveyed by your biography, not your resume, and should be directed specifically to hiring managers in companies that are of interest to you.

In drafting your biography, pretend that one of those hiring managers has asked you the question:

"How can you help our company?"

The answer you give, which should include a blend of your skills, experience, expertise, and style, is what goes down on paper and becomes your biography. Then flip it around to third person. Your biography characterizes the value you offer moving forward, while your resume is nothing more than a track record of past positions, postings, and employment. From the employer's perspective, your value always trumps your resume.

TACTIC #7—INITIATE A DIALOG

Depending on the situation, there are two cover letters that accompany your biography when introducing yourself directly to a hiring manager:

The **Strategic Value letter** and the
Strategic Job Listing letter

Samples of these two letters can be found in Chapter 3 of this book.

The Strategic Value Letter

The **Strategic Value letter** is sent to a hiring manager in a company where there are no apparent openings at all. In this scenario all you are aiming to do is to introduce yourself to the hiring manager, with your bio, to give him/her a teaser of your background. As the letter states, you are not looking for a job.

You then follow up several days later with a phone call to answer any questions he or she may have about your background and to restate your confidence that at some point in the future you could bring added value to the company. Then ask if you can stay in touch, perhaps connecting once a month or so through e-mail or LinkedIn, so that "should an opportunity open up in the future where I could bring added-value perhaps we could get together and talk about it."

When you make your follow-up call to the hiring manager, several days after mailing your biography and cover letter, you'll experience one of several scenarios:

Follow-Up Call to Strategic Value Letter

If you get sent to voice mail, leave a brief message and give a time window to let the manager know when you will be calling again. Invite the manager to call you and leave your phone number, for example:

"Hello Mr. Jones. This is John Smith calling and I'm following up on some information I forwarded to you several days ago. I'm sorry I missed you; however I will try again tomorrow between 9 a.m. and noon. In the meantime, if you have the opportunity to call me I can be reached at (555) 555-5555. I look forward to speaking with you."

If you're fortunate enough to be connected directly to the hiring manager, the typical conversation may be:

"Hi John, I got your information and looked at your background. There's nothing for you here. Sorry, I can't help you."

Instead of saying "thank you" and hanging up, your response should be something like this:

"I understand Mr. Jones, and I appreciate you taking my call anyway. As I mentioned in my letter I certainly didn't expect there to be any opportunities for me at the moment. I simply wanted to take a couple of minutes to introduce myself to you, give you an overview of my background, and to

let you know that I'm confident that at some point in the future I could bring added value to you and your company. Would it be okay if I could stay in touch with you, perhaps sending you an e-mail once a month or so or staying connected through LinkedIn, so that should something open up in the future perhaps we could sit down and talk about it?"

Nine times out of ten the hiring manager will say yes to you staying in touch. Once in awhile you'll get someone who tells you to get the heck out of his life, but you wouldn't want to go to work there anyway.

On the other hand, you may have a meaningful conversation about your background and the potential value you offer. The hiring manager may even ask for your resume. At this point this is the best outcome since it appears there is genuine interest. Now you know your resume is going directly to the hiring manager, the one person who can truly appreciate what you can potentially bring to the table, and your resume will get the attention it deserves.

Follow-up E-mail

After talking with your target, it is prudent to send a periodic e-mail. **Do not start** the process with an e-mail. Only send an e-mail when you have permission from the recipient! Otherwise, it could be considered spam.

So let's say you have successfully had a real conversation but no opportunities may exist at the moment. At least you've established a good dialog with the hiring manager and a very valid reason to stay in touch by sending a simple e-mail once a month or so, for example:

Good morning Mr. Jones,

You may remember we spoke a month or so ago about my background in project management and my interest in your company. I just wanted to let you know that I enjoy staying in touch. Please let me know if there is anything I can do to help you moving forward.

All the best, John Smith

You want to use any excuse you can find to send the hiring manager an e-mail. Here is a potential example:

Hi Mr. Jones,

You may remember we spoke a month or so ago about my background in project management and my interest in your company. I noticed last week's article in the Business Journal *about your recent growth and third-quarter earnings, which were above expectations. Congratulations. Please let me know if there is anything I can do to help you moving forward.*

All the best, John Smith.

The Strategic Job Listing Letter

The **Strategic Job Listing letter** is used when you are responding to a specific job posting.

In this scenario you send your resume and standard cover letter to HR, as requested in the job posting, but at the same time see if you can identify the hiring manager who would oversee that position. Then you send your biography and this letter directly to him/her, with a follow-up phone call to set up a meeting. Don't send your resume to the hiring manager since it will just be forwarded on to HR.

With this approach, when you make your follow-up telephone call to the hiring manager you'll experience one of two typical scenarios:

Success Tip: Use a clear phone line, preferably a land line, to minimize static or the call being dropped.

Telephone Follow-Up

If you get voice mail, leave a brief message and give a time window to let the manager know when you will be calling again. Invite the manager to call you and leave your phone number. For example:

Hello, Ms. Williams. This is John Smith calling and I'm following up on some information I forwarded to you several days ago with regard to my qualifications for the senior project manager position. I'm sorry I missed you. I will try again tomorrow between 9 a.m. and noon. In the meantime, if you have the opportunity to call me I can be reached at (555) 555-5555. I look forward to speaking with you.

If you're fortunate enough to be connected directly to the hiring manager, your conversation could begin with:

Hello, Ms. Williams. This is John Smith calling and I'm following up on some information I forwarded to you several days ago with regard to my qualifications for the senior project manager position. As I mentioned in my letter, I have forwarded my resume directly to your human resources department. However, as you and I both know it's probably buried in a stack a foot high. My concern is that my value is buried in that stack and that's why I'm contacting you directly.

When you forward your biography and cover letter to your targeted hiring managers **don't use e-mail**. A busy manager gets a hundred e-mails a day and with a simple click of the mouse you're gone, along with your potential value.

Instead, go to the post office and send your biography and cover letter by Priority Mail. In two to three days it will arrive in a flat, red-white-and-blue Priority Mail envelope that will create a sense of urgency. Odds are it will be placed right on the hiring manager's desk. It will cost you a few dollars but well worth it. Remember, the goal is to get noticed by the right person and Priority Mail should help!

Regardless of whether you're using the Strategic Value letter or the Strategic Job Listing letter be sure to manage your activity in terms of following up as indicated in your correspondence. The key is to follow up promptly so your information is still fresh in the hiring manager's mind.

The Biography

When properly used, your biography offers six distinct advantages over your resume:

 With your biography you can promote yourself any way you want. Remember, your resume is very restrictive in its format. You have to include where you worked, how long you worked there, what you did, how long you did it, and your educational background. With your resume there's no way to avoid providing that information.

 Your biography avoids the pitfalls of the resume format. Resumes are typically presented in chronological format, functional format, or a combination of both. The entire document is related to the past and you are severely limited in how you can present yourself.

❸ You can customize your selling approach to prospective employers **before** submitting a resume. This is a huge advantage because with your biography you can address specific areas where you can add value to a particular organization moving forward, whereas your resume is nothing more than a reflection of the past.

❹ Your biography avoids HR department personnel completely. Since it's sent directly to key decision-makers, your biography never goes anywhere near human resources. They wouldn't know what to do with it anyway since it doesn't look like a resume.

5 Your biography has more credibility. Your approach with your biography is more believable since it's tailored to a specific situation or company. Your resume is just a track record of employment.

And, most important…

6 Your biography differentiates you from 99 percent of all other job seekers. While others are relying on a powerful resume and knock-'em-dead cover letter to get them noticed by some personnel jockey, you're working smarter, not harder. You're making an end run around the masses and differentiating yourself by targeting the hiring manager—the one person who can truly appreciate the potential value you offer. You're standing out from the crowd!

Effective Use of your Biography

You can use your biography in a variety of different ways:

- Personal networking—updating friends and relatives about your background while informing them of your career transition.

- Professional networking—staying connected, or reconnecting, with former coworkers and people you meet at various networking groups, industry associations, etc., during and after your job search.

- Targeting companies—the most effective way to educate the business community and get the attention of hiring managers in companies of interest.

CHAPTER EIGHT

Using Social Networks in Your Job Hunt

Remember that your biggest challenge in your job search is differentiation. How do you separate yourself from all other job seekers in a highly competitive job market?

As you continue to encounter the challenges of career transition, increase your odds by creating your own unique identity in the job market.

You must become a unique brand.

This nontraditional approach will help separate you from your competition but it requires some hard work.

Use your biography to convey the value you represent to the business community. With this approach you'll be **creating opportunity** instead of spending the majority of your time chasing posted jobs and just **waiting for opportunity**.

An essential tactic in your new strategy to market yourself instead of your resume is to use the social networking tool LinkedIn.

AN INTRODUCTION TO LINKEDIN

LinkedIn is a social network designed for business professionals. Its name tells what it was designed for—linking professionals with each other. Think of Facebook as a family picnic where you catch up with friends and family, while LinkedIn is more like a business chamber mixer. Members expect to do business with other members and help find qualified job applicants.

This business-like mentality is important to keep in mind when creating your LinkedIn profile, adding updates, seeking introductions to new contacts, joining LinkedIn groups (a very powerful resource) and so on. Rather than offer cutesy games and tons of spam, LinkedIn is geared specifically to professionals as a source of information and introductions.

Most Fortune 500 executives are on LinkedIn. There are also company profiles to help you do research on the company's locations, officers, size, and especially anyone you know inside! Used properly, LinkedIn is a job seeker's best resource.

Creating Your LinkedIn Profile

Signing up for and using basic LinkedIn is free to users. The site does have some advertising, but it's unobtrusive and often job related. All you need to get started is to go to http://www.LinkedIn.com and create a LinkedIn login to sign up for a free account.

Once you sign up for a LinkedIn account, you can create your own professional profile. Your photograph (also known as your avatar) should be a clear and compelling head shot and not the funky chicken costume you wore for Halloween. It will pay to have a good professional photographer do a series of photographs for your social media needs!

This profile is your chance to post your **biography**! You explain who you are and what you offer to other members of the LinkedIn community. Use keywords to describe who you are and what you can do for your target industries or companies.

Gregory S. Wood, CCMP

Founder of The Hire Challenge™, Creator of TheHireRoad™, Author of The Hire Advantage™,
Co-Author of The Hire Tactics™

gregw@thehireroad.com

Summary

Certified Career Management Professional, author, speaker and trainer with extensive experience working with professionals and veterans in career transition, both individually and in outplacement environments.

SPECIFIC EXPERTISE: Helping job seekers avoid the traditional system of finding employment that has turned to C*R*A*P (Clicking, Reviewing, Applying, Praying).

Authored The Hire Advantage™ in 2013, based on the four key milestones in TheHireRoad™. These four milestones take job seekers step-by-step through the entire job search process, introducing innovative tools, resources and strategies to help them achieve critical differentiation. This unique job search methodology, modified specifically for veterans, is available in The Hire Tactics™ (co-authored in 2013 by Tom Stein, USMC Retired).

Created TheHireRoad™ methodology in 2002, introducing the company's flagship product, TheHireRoad™, in early 2006. This innovative CD-based job search tutorial has been well received by job seekers and the HR community alike. TheHireRoad™ College Graduate Version was introduced in late 2008.

TheHireRoad™ teaches an entirely different methodology to meet the challenges of job search. The traditional system of finding employment, which relies on mass distribution of "powerful resumes" and "knock 'em dead cover letters" no longer works. With TheHireRoad™ job seekers learn how to create their own unique identity in the job market by going beyond their resume, broadcasting their value to the business community, and connecting directly with hiring managers.

My personal goal is to continue to emphasize the importance of a strategic vs. traditional approach to job search. Things have changed, times have changed, and times are tough. Successful job search requires a change in mindset and a willingness to pursue and implement a more effective approach to finding employment.

Specialties: Strategic vs. traditional job search

Experience

Founder at The Hire Challenge™
May 2011 - Present (2 years 4 months)

The Hire Challenge™ provides a range of career transition services for both civilians and veterans, including a series of books on strategic vs. traditional job search based on TheHireRoad™, the highly successful

Page1

79

CD-based job search tutorial. Company also provides affordable one-on-one career transition support to individuals as well as providing corporate outplacement services.

Creator, at TheHireRoad™ CD-based Job Search Tutorial
July 2005 - Present (8 years 2 months)

Tired of the same old outdated methodology for job search? TheHireRoad™ is a unique career transition support program that teaches a strategic vs. traditional approach to finding employment. This proven program introduces innovative tools, resources and strategies to help job seekers achieve critical differentiation in today's highly competitive job market and shorten their time in transition.

5 recommendations available upon request

Facilitator at Paradise Cafe Job Club
2011 - 2013 (2 years)

Career Consultant at Women's Opportunities Center - UCI
2005 - 2010 (5 years)

Volunteer position which included conducting a variety of workshops on strategic job search and working with individuals in transition. Also facilitated a job club on a rotating basis every third month.

Career Consultant at Executive Career Services
2003 - 2006 (3 years)

Provided individual career counseling services to professionals in transition and conducted a variety of job search related workshops.

Owner at G. S. Wood & Associates
February 2001 - June 2005 (4 years 5 months)

Provided career counseling and executive search services to professionals in transition.

Recruiter at Management Recruiters International
1996 - 1997 (1 year)

VP of Sales & Marketing at Genesis Clinical Laboratory
1993 - 1996 (3 years)

Account Executive at Terrano Corporation
1992 - 1993 (1 year)

General Manager at FastFacts - Murdoch Magazines
1984 - 1990 (6 years)

VP Sales & Marketing at MetPath Inc. / MetPath U.K. Limited
June 1975 - August 1984 (9 years 3 months)

Senior sales and marketing roles for MetPath, Inc. and MetPath U.K. Limited. MetPath, Inc. was acquired by Corning in 1981 and is now Quest Diagnositcs.

Page2

Publications

The Hire Advantage
Peterson's / Nelnet   June 19, 2013
Authors: Gregory S. Wood, CCMP

Based on the four key milestones in TheHireRoad™, the highly successful CD-based job search tutorial, The Hire Advantage™ provides specific and innovative strategies to gain employment in today's new economy. Unlike other job search resources, The Hire Advantage™ introduces you to unique tools that are designed to convey your value to the business community while clearly differentiating yourself from the competition.

The Hire Tactics™
Peterson's / Nelnet   July 14, 2013
Authors: Gregory S. Wood, CCMP

Based on The Hire Advantage™ job search methodology for civilians, The Hire Tactics™ is specifically dedicated to help military veterans succeed in their search for employment. Unlike other job search resources, you'll learn how the system really works, how to use your tactical advantage as a veteran, and how to succeed in your job search mission. Co-authored with Tom Stein, USMC Retired.

Skills & Expertise

Resume Writing
Coaching
Negotiation
Public Speaking
Mentoring
Writing
Sales Management
Career Counseling
Executive Coaching
Job Search
Interviews
Leadership Development
Cover Letters
Career Management
Career Development
Outplacement
Interview Preparation
Executive Search
Team Building
Management
Recruiting
Talent Management
Strategy
Leadership
Personal Branding

Page3

Training
Business Networking
Time Management
Job Coaching
Consulting
Workshop Facilitation
Motivational Speaking
Job Search Strategies
Organizational Development
Employee Training
Organizational Effectiveness
Personal Development
MBTI
Life Coaching
Executive Development
Emotional Intelligence
Conflict Resolution
360 Feedback
Business Coaching

Education

University of Portland
BBA, Marketing, 1964 - 1969

Interests

Career coaching, professional networking, public speaking, reading and travel.

Gregory S. Wood, CCMP

Founder of The Hire Challenge™, Creator of TheHireRoad™, Author of The Hire Advantage™, Co-Author of The Hire Tactics™

gregw@thehireroad.com

Linked in.

5 people have recommended Gregory S.

"Greg Wood gave a professional and insightful presentation to the Eloy Job Club. I first heard him at Career Connectors and invited him to our group. I value his words since it was obvious that his method works. Our participants learned much from him and he patiently answered all their questions and acknowledged their experiences.. I am planning to have them all do their biographies the next time we meet. TheHireChallenge.com is truly an asset to the unemployed. I highly recommend Mr. Wood."

— **Socorro Galusha Luna**, was Gregory S.'s client

"Greg Wood of TheHireRoad is not just another consultant who advises you on how to customize your cover letter and resume and then checks the spelling and grammar. Greg shares a proven strategy that works in getting in touch with the right people to obtain a job even in a tough employment market. His tips on how to prepare for the questions that may be asked and the information you should ask during an interview are the keys in maximizing valuable interview time. His simple steps in following up after interviews are essential in differentiating yourself from other candidates seeking the same position. His one on one consulting enables you to customize several points into a search strategy that fits your personality and the position you are seeking. People that can help seem far and few between when you are in job transition and need assistance. Greg Wood is there to help when it is needed the most. Doug Burchard Residential & Commercial Mortgage Consultant Certified Commercial Investment Member CCIM National Mortgage Lending Originator Calif. Real Estate Broker Linkedin.com/in/dougburchard"

— **Doug Burchard, CCIM, GRI**, was Gregory S.'s client

"Mr. Wood is by far the best career planner I have ever had the pleasure to work with. I met Greg several years ago when I decided to make a transition to another career field. With the use of his "HireRoad" methodology and tools, I have attained a senior executive position as a College President in Southern California. "TheHireRoad" provided me the path to achieve my personal and professional goals. I now have partnered with Greg to help US Marines and other veterans who are making the transition from a military career to the corporate world. He is a great American!"

— **Tom Stein**, *Senior Program Manager, Programs: IS and BCP Programs, Ingram Micro*, worked with Gregory S. at TheHireRoad, LLC

"I had the pleasure to work with Greg through the Women's Opportunity Center, Career and Life Planning

Page5

Program at UCI Extension. I have successfully used Greg's innovative and effective strategic ideas for professionals in transition. Greg is an excellent teacher and an inspirational role model. He is empowering while sharing his knowledge and motivates job seekers to test his unique techniques in real life. Greg has been a great supporter throughout the process, providing practical advice and hope. I highly recommend Greg's services to all on the road to success."

— **Klara Detrano**, was Gregory S.'s client

"Greg is quite the best career coach I have ever met. Great ideas, helpful manner. Great CD series, too. Highly recommended."

— **Glenn Baxter**, was Gregory S.'s client

Contact Gregory S. on LinkedIn

Remember, since this is a professionally-oriented website, it's important that information in your profile represents your business or working side. LinkedIn is not the place to share cute baby photos or show how drunk you got at last week's party. My social media advisors recommend you review the profile of other members in your industry to see how they structure their descriptions.

Some of the things you can add to a profile include the basics of your resume, a summary about yourself, your contact information, links to your website and/or blog, your Twitter account, and more.

Once your profile is ready, you publish it and start looking for connections. A connection is a person that you know or would like to know more about on LinkedIn. Essentially the idea is to create as many direct connections as you can by adding people within your own professional circle and branching out to include their connections. Do not connect to people you do not know directly. You can get penalized for doing that too many times.

Your connections can also provide introductions to other professionals you might be interested in meeting. Connections can also provide you with standing recommendations for employment.

Success Tip: Do **not** invite all your contacts to be your LinkedIn friend at one time! Ignore the offer to import all your contacts when you first set up your LinkedIn account. Choose the individuals for whom LinkedIn fits their needs and profile. Then invite them individually with a **personalized** invitation. Explain why you think it is a good idea they link to you.

How LinkedIn Can Help You

LinkedIn allows you to:

- Get online recommendations for your professional abilities and your character.

- Get introductions to potential employers or colleagues in your field.

- Search available job postings placed on the LinkedIn website by members and member companies. You can search by job type, location, or company name.

While you can also search the web for jobs through LinkedIn, the big benefit is that many job posts are exclusive to LinkedIn and aren't advertised elsewhere. In addition, there is a chance that someone within your LinkedIn network already works there or knows someone who does, giving you a big foot in the door for an interview.

One way to accelerate your link building is to join various groups that align with your interests and participate in discussions. Having a group in common with another LinkedIn user is one way you can invite others into your network. Each group discussion contains its own job listings. Be helpful to other group members and **don't sell**. Ask for help and offer help.

You can create an online resume that mirrors your paper resume. LinkedIn allows hiring companies and recruiters to search for professionals who might fit their criteria. The secret to resume success on LinkedIn is knowing the common keywords for job candidates in that field. You learn those by reviewing job descriptions and the company profiles posted on LinkedIn.

SECTION 3

52 Job Interview Questions You Need to Know!

INTRODUCTION

So you've gotten past the HR sensors. You've successfully networked your biography onto a hiring manager's desk. It's now time to impress your future employer face-to-face. I created a unique in-home job search system that provides you with direction for success in your job transition. One of the most popular parts of TheHireRoad™ is the collection of 84 interview questions you are likely to be asked during a job interview, including questions you should consider asking the interviewer in return. Fifty-two of these questions are included in this section. Job seekers use these questions to prepare and rehearse for the interview where they will hopefully seal the deal and be offered a job.

You need to learn and practice your skills for this critical part of the job search process! You **must** rehearse your interview answers.

As you begin to prepare for your upcoming interview, remember that you have a choice. This is the **same** choice you had when you began your job search. You can follow the traditional approach, which is **reactive**, or you can choose to differentiate yourself by being **strategically proactive.**

Why is this difference important? Let me take a minute to talk about interviewing from both a traditional and strategic perspective.

Think about the reason you've been selected to come in and interview. It's not because you're a nice person who's out of work and needs a paycheck. It's because the hiring manager has problems and issues that need to be solved. By solving those problems, the hiring manager looks good, the department looks good, and profitability will be enhanced. The hiring manager has looked at your background, has determined that you represent a solution to his problems, and wants to consider hiring you. Your employment is all about solving problems.

When you're invited in to interview, it's important to remember that you're 80 percent of the way there. The hiring manager knows you can do the job; it's right there on your resume. However, if you're one of five candidates interviewing for the same job, you **all** represent solutions to the problems at hand.

The manager's challenge is to determine who is the best fit. It's this remaining 20 percent, this fit, that will drive his or her decision to select one candidate over another. Are you going to be able to work well with your new boss and a new team? And are you the type of person who will mesh with the culture and environment of the company?

> *YOUR challenge is to convince the hiring manager that YOU are the BEST fit and her best candidate, that you are her PREFERRED SOLUTION to her employee hiring problem.*

The vast majority of job seekers go into a traditional interview with two key emotions: anxiety and fear. They suffer from anxiety because they don't know what questions are going to be asked and if they can answer them in a professional way. They also have a fear of rejection. They know they're competing with others for the same job and they want to be the one chosen. Their whole approach is reactive. They nervously clutch their resume with beads of sweat forming on their forehead, wait for the same questions that the hiring manager asks of each candidate, and rely on their past experience to get them the job. They fail to connect with the interviewer, fail to achieve differentiation, and therefore look like every other candidate.

The chemistry you're able to establish between you and the hiring manager is essential in moving the process forward to an offer. And that chemistry begins the moment you walk in the manager's office. It's here where your choice to conduct a proactive and strategic interview will differentiate you from your competition.

As you begin thinking about your upcoming interview, keep in mind these important points about hiring managers:

First, the majority of hiring managers dislike interviewing. They would rather get back to their regular job.

Second, the vast majority of hiring managers don't have a clue about how to conduct an effective interview. Why? Because they haven't been trained. Many make their hiring decisions based on a popularity contest, rather than choosing the candidate who can best solve the problems and issues that will help increase profitability.

The purpose of the interview, from both your perspective and that of the hiring manager, should be a discussion of the work at hand. However, since most hiring managers are poorly prepared they conduct nothing more than standard interrogations, asking the same questions of each candidate.

Even though you're going to be conducting a strategic interview and taking subtle control, you will still be quizzed about a variety of topics unrelated to the job.

CHAPTER NINE

10 Steps for Preparing for Your Strategic Interview

If you used the tactics outlined earlier in the book you should be preparing for your first interview. This section is all about nailing the interview and getting that job. To help maximize your chances for success, here are ten simple steps to follow in preparing for a strategic interview:

Step 1—If you have the option, try to have the interview scheduled at a time of day when you're at your best. Are you rested and energetic in the morning, after lunch, or do you have increased energy late in the day?

Step 2—Review the questions I provide in this book, review my suggested answer to each question, and then rephrase it as you would answer those questions in the interview. Then get comfortable with your responses by practicing with a friend.

Step 3—Having researched the company (prior to the day of your interview), be fully prepared with several questions concerning the company in general, and several more relating to the specific job you're interviewing for. Write them down on the legal pad you'll be using for making notes during the entire interview. Asking relevant questions during the interview makes you **proactive** and will differentiate you from other candidates. Remember, your competition will be **reactive**, clutching a sweat-soaked resume.

Step 4—Get into the mindset that you are a professional first and someone else's employee second. Don't forget, the hiring manager needs your help to solve their problems. You are there as a potential problem-solver and not just a job holder.

Step 5—Don't refer to your resume; you can't rely on it to get you the job. If the hiring manager asks you about your background or something specific on the resume, make sure you are prepared to tell a story behind whatever accomplishments you've included on your resume.

Step 6—Treat the interview as a **business meeting.** You are there to learn more about their problems and demonstrate how you can solve them! You're going to try and initiate a conversation with the hiring manager, not just sit there and wait for question after question after question.

Step 7—With the business meeting mentality in mind, be ready with questions that will uncover the hiring manager's problems and issues, and use examples from your past experience that highlight your strengths as they apply to solving those problems.

Step 8—Be prepared to relate how your experience brings value to the organization and how it will enhance profitability.

Step 9—Prepare to go into your business meeting and act like an **employee**, not a candidate. This is the best advice I can give you.

Step 10—Read this book and rehearse on the way to the interview to help you remember suggested responses to key questions.

The more questions you rehearse the better. While the 52 questions in this book may seem like a lot, TheHireRoad™ system actually includes an audio CD with 84 questions to help you rehearse and prepare for your interviews. The more questions you know, the more likely you are to maximize your chances for success.

Just to show you how specialized preparation for interviews must be, I have co-written a book focused on questions for military veterans, including the disabled (www.TheHireTactics.com). There's also an audio CD of interview questions designed for college graduates.

CHAPTER TEN

Personal Questions

Personal questions are generally asked by the hiring manager to put both of you at ease as the interview begins. They can be very simple, such as asking if you would like something to drink, referring to a particular news story, the weather, or a sporting event. In this initial exchange it's important that you stay away from anything controversial. A good rule of thumb is no politics, religion, or sexual issues! This is a **business** meeting and not a social event.

Here are some personal inquiries a hiring manager may use to understand more about you as an individual, and, therefore, your potential fit within the organization.

QUESTION 1—TELL ME ABOUT YOURSELF.

This is usually the first question asked at the outset of any interview to help put you at ease. It's where you begin to connect with the hiring manager and establish the chemistry that's so important to your successful interview. If you're not prepared, this question may make you uncomfortable. Still, such an open invitation can be a significant benefit to you because it's a great opportunity to convey some important points about you, prior to the nitty-gritty of the interview.

Since this is an open-ended inquiry, be careful not to ramble or share too much information. To answer succinctly you need to stick to professional information rather than delve deep into personal facts. Why? Because some companies use this open-ended question to let you volunteer personal information they are forbidden by law to ask, such as marital status or sexual orientation!

So when you hear "tell me about yourself," your reply should be, *"You mean on a professional level, correct?"*

The answer you get will give you the direction to follow. While 95 percent of the time the interest will be in your professional background, occasionally the interest will be personal or it could be both. In this case, you need to be careful as to what personal information you disclose.

After you clarify the information the hiring manager seeks from the question, you'll want to ensure your response encompasses four key components.

1 State your expertise in present tense. Remember, your expertise is current and didn't end when you left your last employer. For example, *"I am a Senior Project Manager."*

2 Give a brief summary of your career. This summary is not a recitation of your resume but a narrative that provides the hiring manager with an overview. For example, *"My background includes more than 10 years experience in the telecommunications industry. But let me take a step back and tell you how I got to where I am today."* As you briefly describe your career, try to mention one or two accomplishments by telling a story that highlights your strengths.

3 After bringing the hiring manager back up to present day, explain the reason you left (are leaving) your last employer. This takes that question off the table and lets you address it as a historical fact instead of a defensive answer. For example, *"And the reason I'm no longer with XYZ Company (or the reason I am looking for a new position) is due to . . . ."* You can now insert your reason such as a major restructuring, your position being eliminated, desire to move/stay in the area, etc.

4 The fourth and final component is what I call "painting a picture." You conclude your response by stating what you're looking to do moving forward. For example,

> *"What I'm looking to do now is to join a progressive company that will take full advantage of my project management skills, an organization where I can continue to grow professionally for the long term, make a substantial contribution to the success of the company, and be fairly compensated for my efforts. I'm hoping that's the kind of opportunity that we'll be discussing today."*

QUESTION 2—WHY ARE YOU NO LONGER WITH XYZ CORPORATION?

When explaining why you're no longer with your former employer, always tell the truth and give the same reason you gave to others. Don't take the chance that people in your network may provide conflicting information.

There can be many legitimate reasons why you left your former employer. These could include downsizing due to economic conditions, a restructuring, outsourcing of job functions, relocation of the company itself, a merger or acquisition, or the company going out of business. It could also be interpersonal issues with supervisors or team members that cause you to leave voluntarily. Maybe you simply wanted a new direction for your career!

Whatever the reason, avoid using the words "terminated" or "fired" or any other words that have a negative connotation. Try to stay positive about why you are interviewing with this particular company. Be truthful without being judgmental!

"The company underwent a major restructuring and my position was eliminated."

OR

"My division was consolidated with corporate headquarters back east and relocation was not practical."

OR

"The company merged and new management came in with their own team, creating job redundancy."

OR

"The company was no longer a good fit based on their needs and my skills."

QUESTION 3—WHY ARE YOU THINKING OF LEAVING XYZ CORPORATION?

If your resume reflects current employment, anticipate this question being asked and prepare your response carefully. Make sure you tell the truth and give the same reason you gave to others. Don't take the chance that people in your network may provide conflicting information. There are many reasons why you may be thinking of leaving your present company. Here are a few suggested responses that may apply to your situation.

"After new management came in, they changed my job responsibilities, which affected my ability to continue to grow professionally within the organization."

OR

"My manager and I had different philosophies, which prevented me from performing to the best of my ability."

OR

"While I really enjoy working at my present company, my spouse has been transferred to another state."

While you may actually be thinking of leaving your job because you're bored stiff, you can't stand your manager, or you don't enjoy the 2-hour commute each way, make sure that whatever reason you give does not have a negative tone. The examples I just gave are neutral and can fit many situations.

QUESTION 4—WHAT DID YOU ENJOY THE MOST ABOUT YOUR LAST JOB?

If you left your last company involuntarily, respond positively and explain that you enjoyed everything about your job. Focus on those responsibilities you had that reflect your strengths and try to relate them to the job you're currently interviewing for.

If you're still employed, again you want to talk about the responsibilities you currently have that tie in with the job you're applying for. Talk about those enjoyable aspects of your work that bring out your strengths. Did you enjoy being a project manager? Were you an ace at leading your team to new sales goals? Then talk about those positive experiences. Emphasize that this position you're now exploring gives you an even greater opportunity to demonstrate those strengths.

QUESTION 5—WHAT DID YOU ENJOY THE LEAST ABOUT YOUR LAST JOB?

This is a tricky question, so let me suggest how NOT to respond. Don't say something like, *"Well, I didn't like working 14 hours a day,"* or *"I was never given the resources necessary to do the job,"* or *"My manager never fully explained what my responsibilities were day to day."*

These kind of responses are all negative in their tone, and they may reveal personal characteristics that could screen you out. The hiring manager may interpret your responses to mean that you're not fully committed to your work, you lack resourcefulness, or you find it difficult to work independently and make decisions on your own.

Your response needs to have a positive spin. You may want to mention a situation on your last job where you had to accept things as they were instead of what you would have liked them to be. Such a situation could have inhibited your professional growth within the company. Or, your response could acknowledge one aspect of your job that you disliked, such as routine paperwork. For example, you may say, *"Well, I understand the necessity of generating reports for senior management, but I am very much a hands-on person and I don't enjoy being bogged down with paperwork."*

QUESTION 6—WHAT DO YOU LOOK FOR IN YOUR "IDEAL" JOB?

This is an open-ended question that allows you to focus on the importance of "fit" from both your perspective and the company's. Your response should refer to the value you bring to the company and the benefits of working for that company.

Here are some possible responses:

"I'm looking for an opportunity where I can continue to grow professionally in a challenging work environment. I don't like to get bored with my work."

OR

"I believe teamwork is the most important characteristic of any successful company. I thrive in a team environment where everybody is committed to achieving a common goal."

OR

"My ideal job is one that's dynamic, with responsibilities that are continually evolving and that allows me to continue to grow professionally and enhance my value to the organization by making the maximum contribution."

QUESTION 7—WHY DO YOU WANT TO COME TO WORK FOR OUR COMPANY?

This question allows you to respond in a way that shows you've done your research. Mention two or three positive aspects about the company that appeal to you. For example, the industry they're in, the company's innovative products, or their history of growth. You can also refer to information you discovered about the job itself, the culture of the company, and how such an environment would allow you to maximize your contribution.

Your response could be, *"I'm interested in your company for several reasons. Not only do you have an impressive history of growth in the industry over the last few years, but you're also developing leading-edge products that represent a potential increase in market share. My research has also identified several challenges that you're currently facing, challenges where my skills, experience and expertise could be of significant value. I feel that joining your company would be to our mutual benefit."*

QUESTION 8—WHAT PROFESSIONAL ACCOMPLISHMENTS ARE YOU MOST PROUD OF?

Choose accomplishments that relate to the job you're applying for. Explain how the experiences you've gained through these accomplishments enable you to face similar situations in the future.

For example, if you're applying for a Senior Project Manager position, your response may be, *"One of my proudest accomplishments was when I was with XYZ Company. I completed a major project six weeks ahead of schedule and $400,000 under budget. Up until that time, I had only managed smaller projects. Now I have the confidence to handle a project of almost any size."*

QUESTION 9—WHAT DO YOU CONSIDER YOUR MAJOR STRENGTHS?

This question is almost always asked during the interview along with the weakness question. Aside from mentioning the obvious, such as your interpersonal skills, talk about your strengths as they relate to the job you're currently interviewing for. Here's where having a job description *before* the interview is imperative. Focus your strengths on those that are reflected in the description.

Make sure you have written those on your notepad for quick reference if you need to have a reminder handy.

QUESTION 10—WHAT DO YOU CONSIDER YOUR GREATEST WEAKNESS?

This question is almost always asked by the hiring manager and, for some reason, is one of the most feared by the candidate. But it doesn't have to be if you're prepared. In my opinion, it's one of the top five dumb questions that can be asked in an interview.

Why?

Because it has nothing to do with the problems and issues faced by the hiring manager. The manager's not interested in your actual weaknesses, but how you respond to the question. What's important to note is that most hiring managers can see right through standard responses, such as "I'm a perfectionist," or "I'm a workaholic and tend to spend too much time at the office."

Whatever weakness you choose, make sure that you put a positive spin on it. An easy way to remember how best to respond is the Oreo cookie example. The dark cookie on top is a positive statement about you, the white filling is your perceived weakness, and the dark cookie on the bottom is another positive statement.

For example, *"Well, throughout my career, I have worked many times in a team environment and I'm very committed to my work. I like to see projects done on time and under budget. However, I have to tell you, sometimes I get very frustrated with other team members who tend to drag their feet and don't share that same kind of commitment. I like working with people who are highly motivated like I am and share a common pursuit of excellence in their work."*

In this response, you began by mentioning one of your strengths—how committed you are to your work (the dark cookie on top). You then mention your perceived weakness—your frustration with others who don't share the same commitment (the white filling), and then you end with another positive statement—your motivation and pursuit of excellence (the dark cookie on the bottom). If stated correctly, your strengths will overshadow whatever weakness you mentioned.

Another example that can apply to almost anyone is a technical weakness. Your response may be, *"I would consider one of my weaknesses actually to be technical. While I'm very proficient in Microsoft Word and Excel, I'm not that strong in PowerPoint, which is one tool that could help me improve my presentation skills. So, therefore, I've enrolled in a local community college and in a couple of months I'll be proficient in PowerPoint."*

QUESTION 11—DO YOU PREFER TO WORK ALONE OR WORK IN A TEAM ENVIRONMENT?

Your response needs to stress the fact that you believe that teamwork is the most important contributor to a company's success. You need to let them know when you genuinely prefer to work in a team environment. While your position, such as a copywriter or website developer, may require you to work alone, you're still part of a larger team, all focused on a common goal. The important thing to convey here is that you have the ability to work well both independently and in a team environment.

Your response may be, *"I believe teamwork to be the most important component in a company's success. In fact, I believe that the ability to work with others is crucial to succeed not only in your career, but in your life. I've always enjoyed working in a team environment. I do realize, however, that sometimes it's necessary to work independently. It's easy for me to work in both environments and do whatever is necessary to be successful."*

QUESTION 12—WHAT TYPE OF PERSON DO YOU FIND IT DIFFICULT TO WORK WITH?

This is a variation on the "What do you like in a boss/coworker/team member?" question. It is deliberately phrased as a negative to see if you "take the bait" and make negative comments.

When answering this question, you need to be careful not to mention a specific trait that could describe the hiring manager you're interviewing with, i.e., micromanager or hands-off management style. Therefore, keep your response generic. Let me give you a few examples:

"I find it difficult to work with people who are not committed to their work and, basically, only show up for the sake of a paycheck."

OR

"I have difficulty working with people who are loners, who don't enjoy working in a team environment. I believe teamwork is the most important component to success for any organization."

OR

"I have a problem with people who compromise their principles and ethics in a work environment, and take very little pride in what they do."

QUESTION 13—WHERE DO YOU SEE YOURSELF IN FIVE YEARS?

I'm not sure of the relevance of this question in today's job world. But it still seems to be frequently asked in interviews. Hiring managers may like to get an idea of your career plans for the next several years as a way to assess whether or not you are looking for the "long term." However, let's be realistic. Career planning has become career coping. As long as you're working for someone else, your five-year career plan can change in a heartbeat.

A good response is, *"Well, with business and technology changing so rapidly, and the uncertainty of the economy, it's really difficult for me to say exactly where*

I'll be in five years. I can tell you the type of company I'd like to be a part of. One that's progressive, stable, and provides a challenging work environment—a company where I can continue to grow professionally, make a significant contribution, and be compensated fairly for my efforts."

CHAPTER ELEVEN

Knowledge Questions

Companies today are interested in acquiring individuals with both talent and knowledge. Your accumulation of knowledge didn't end when you left school. We are all constantly learning throughout our personal and professional lives. So you want to showcase that you are **constantly learning** so your employer can be **constantly earning** from your efforts!

So how you answer knowledge-related questions will convey your value in terms of your understanding of the industry, the company, and how you are prepared to contribute to the growth of the company. Here are a few questions you may be asked that challenge your knowledge.

QUESTION 14—WHAT DO YOU KNOW ABOUT THIS JOB/ POSITION?

Please make sure you have done some basic information gathering on the company and on the job before taking the interview. Hopefully, you kept the job description or job posting that you reviewed before applying for the job! If you don't recall the job—call Human Resources or Google it to find the details.

It's important that your response not only refers to the necessary skills required for the position, but also to your strengths as they relate directly to those skills. Obviously, your response is going to be unique to the job description and your experience. If there are numerous skills listed, pick the ones that will allow you to point out your corresponding significant strengths. What's important here is that you anticipate this question and be prepared.

QUESTION 15—WHAT DO YOU KNOW ABOUT OUR COMPANY?

Do your homework on the company and maybe even this particular subsidiary or location **before** taking the interview. Having that information will let you differentiate yourself from your competition because most job seekers do not research the company beforehand.

While other candidates may have some very basic knowledge of the company, your response should demonstrate your *thorough* knowledge in terms of the company's history, products, services, customers, competitors, market share, financials, vendors, suppliers, and anything else that is relevant. Such in-depth knowledge will be a clear indication of your interest in the position and the company. This is a great opportunity to ask a follow-up question to your response, which will be unique to the circumstances. I would suggest reviewing press releases, if available, dating back several months.

Your response could be something like this: *"I saw from your press release last month that your merger with XYZ Company finally went through. Obviously, your market share is going to increase substantially. How do you see this increase affecting your department?"*

QUESTION 16—WHAT DO YOU THINK IS OUR COMPANY'S BIGGEST CHALLENGE?

Your research of the company should prepare you for this question. Learn all you can from the company's website, press releases, annual reports, trade publications, and other sources that may help you define what the key challenges are. Stay away from controversial topics. If the CEO is walking around with an ankle bracelet to monitor her whereabouts, you probably don't want to mention this particular problem. While your skills and experience may not necessarily relate, whatever challenge you mention gives you the opportunity to ask how the company is addressing it.

Your response can be: *"Well, I learned that your company has recently entered into a price war with your main competitor. In my opinion, this could represent a pretty significant challenge. How do you see this affecting your market share?"*

QUESTION 17—YOUR BACKGROUND HAS BEEN IN A DIFFERENT INDUSTRY THAN OURS. WHAT SKILLS DO YOU FEEL YOU HAVE THAT QUALIFY YOU FOR THIS POSITION?

Everyone has skills that are transferable from one industry to another. Remember, you've been invited in to interview because the hiring manager needs your help, and, after reviewing your background, has concluded that your skills and experience would be valuable to help solve his or her problems. You're obviously not being interviewed for your industry experience, so focus on those transferable skills that you have as they relate to the specific job at hand.

For example, if you're in sales, you obviously realize that every company needs excellent sales and marketing capabilities, regardless of the product or service being offered.

QUESTION 18—THIS POSITION REQUIRES CERTAIN SKILLS THAT AREN'T REFLECTED ON YOUR RESUME. DO YOU FEEL THAT YOU'RE STILL QUALIFIED FOR THE POSITION?

This is a variation on the different background and skills question. Keep in mind that every job description is basically a wish list. There's no such thing as a perfect candidate who happens to meet every specific skill the position requires. Companies select candidates to interview based on how closely they match the requirements of the position.

Ask the hiring manager to clarify what specific skills he's referring to. Odds are these skills will not be essential to the successful performance of the job. If they were, you wouldn't have been invited in to interview.

Your response could be, *"While I may not have the specific skills you mentioned, I do believe I'm well qualified for this position. I am a fast learner and would certainly be willing to learn whatever is necessary to excel in this position."*

QUESTION 19—WHAT DID YOU LEARN IN SCHOOL THAT YOU FEEL COULD APPLY TO THIS JOB?

The variations on this question include asking about college, certificate programs, military experience, even time in prison! Regardless of how little you have utilized your experience or education in your career so far, your response to this question must include some characteristics that reflect your current work ethic.

Your response could be, *"I think one of the most important things I learned while I was in school was self-discipline. This included how to meet deadlines, how to apply myself in terms of establishing goals and achieving them, and the development of good analytical and problem-solving skills. And another thing I learned was how to multitask, handling several classes while working part-time."*

CHAPTER TWELVE

Situational Questions

Questions that are situational in nature are designed to reveal your traits or past behavior as reflected in your work experience. They help the hiring manager determine if your past qualities are those that would be of value to his or her organization going forward into the future. Here are some examples of situational questions:

QUESTION 20—WHAT ARE ONE OR TWO OF THE MOST CRITICAL ISSUES YOU FACED IN YOUR PREVIOUS POSITION? HOW DID YOU SOLVE THEM?

When answering this question, keep in mind the interviewer is trying to find out your thought processes in addressing key challenges. Don't present dry facts, but rather tell a brief story that highlights your strengths in dealing with those issues. If possible, relate those strengths to the potential challenges in the job for which you're being considered.

QUESTION 21—GIVE ME AN EXAMPLE OF WHEN YOU WERE UNSUCCESSFUL IN YOUR LAST JOB.

This is a challenging question because nobody is comfortable talking about a situation in which they were unsuccessful. Your discomfort is one of the reasons that you are asked this question or variations on it! The interviewer gets to see you react under pressure and learns something negative about you that may help them decide on which candidate is better.

Make sure you don't go into a lot of detail and definitely don't place blame for any failures. Keep it professional, focusing on what you've learned from the experience. Emphasize that you're now better prepared to face similar situations in the future.

Your response may be, *"Well, I'm very hard on myself and once in a while I set goals that are unrealistic. For example, as the lead on a project some years ago, I established deadlines that were not achievable. Since that time, I've become better at prioritizing my workload that has helped me reach my goals in a more realistic timeframe."*

QUESTION 22—TELL ME ABOUT A SITUATION WHEN YOU HAD TO WORK WITH SOMEONE WHO DIDN'T LIKE YOU. HOW DID YOU HANDLE IT?

While you don't expect everyone to like you, you always want to make an effort to get along and build a good working relationship with others. As a professional, you want to keep your focus on the job at hand and don't let personal differences interfere with the team's ability to perform.

An example may be, *"As a sales manager, there were occasions during my career when the chemistry between several account executives and me was not evident. I learned to appreciate what motivated each of these individuals and made every effort to recognize the value they contributed to the entire team. This developed mutual respect and trust and enabled the team to achieve its goals."*

QUESTION 23—TELL ME ABOUT A SITUATION IN YOUR CURRENT OR LAST JOB THAT YOU REALLY GOT EXCITED ABOUT?

This is a great opportunity to tell a story and toot your own horn. Give an example that demonstrates some of your key strengths. For example, you may have been the project lead for a variety of small projects and, because of your success, you were promoted to Project Manager. This new role was exciting because it not only allowed you to further develop your leadership and organizational skills, but also to learn new skills and gain greater visibility in a more challenging environment.

QUESTION 24—CAN YOU GIVE ME AN EXAMPLE OF YOUR APPROACH TO PROBLEM SOLVING?

Your answer to this question should demonstrate your critical-thinking skills in solving problems in a logical way. Use a real-life example of a problem you solved in the past that was related to your work experience.

While the example you may give is unique to you, I would suggest your response resemble something like this: *"Well, the best way to solve a problem is to take a systematic approach. I like to first gather as much information as possible, including asking others for relevant input. This helps me gain a clear understanding of the problem. Then I begin to formulate possible solutions, again inviting input from others. Once I've evaluated each potential solution, I then select the one that, in my judgment, would be the most effective in solving the problem. Let me give you an example ..."*

CHAPTER THIRTEEN

Experience Questions

The decision to hire someone is not solely based on the skills of the candidate, but also on what he or she has *done* with those skills. Remember, you're only effective if you add value. You're not measured by what you **can** do but by what you **deliver.** In today's tough job market no one hires potential; they try to hire guaranteed results.

Your ability to effectively answer experience-related questions will help the hiring manager gain a better understanding of the added value you bring to the organization. Here are some examples.

QUESTION 25—DO YOU PREFER TO DELEGATE OR TAKE ON TASKS ALL BY YOURSELF?

Your answer to this question is going to demonstrate your leadership skills and management style. It's important for you to explain that, as a manager, you understand the capabilities of each member of your team and how they can each contribute to the achievement of team goals.

Your response may be, *"I believe that delegating tasks to those who are capable is essential to the success of working together as a team. By recognizing each team member's capabilities in relation to clearly defined tasks, the work at hand is completed more efficiently and more timely and teamwork is enhanced."*

QUESTION 26—AS A MANAGER, HOW HAVE YOU BUILT SUCCESSFUL TEAMS IN THE PAST?

This is another great opportunity to demonstrate your leadership skills and your complete understanding of how teamwork is the foundation of any company's success. Your response may be, *"As a manager, I've always felt that, in order to be successful, I need to surround myself with successful people. Team building requires clear communication of both individual and common goals, an understanding of what motivates each individual team member, and definition of each team member's responsibility to each other. It also requires me, as a manager, to be a hands-on resource to the team and lead by example."*

QUESTION 27—HAVE YOU EVER HAD TO FIRE SOMEONE? WHAT WERE THE CIRCUMSTANCES?

If you've ever had to fire someone, briefly explain the situation but be sure to mention that terminating someone, although sometimes necessary, is never something you enjoy doing.

Your response may be, *"Yes, I have had to fire people and it never is a pleasant experience. I once had a situation where I had to let a team member go for performance issues. The individual was placed on probation and given every opportunity to improve performance. However, the situation did not improve and began to affect the morale of other team members as well as their overall performance."*

QUESTION 28—WHEN YOU HIRE SOMEONE, WHAT DO YOU LOOK FOR IN A SUCCESSFUL CANDIDATE?

The interviewer is giving you a chance to outline what they should look for in you and your fellow candidates! This can help you position yourself by giving the employer a yardstick that fits you best.

That said, a successful candidate for any position requires three key components: the skills to do the job, the willingness to do the job, and the ability to fit in well with the organization. The fit is the most important of these components. As you answer this question, keep in mind that the hiring manager is evaluating you from exactly the same perspective.

Your response may be, *"While candidates obviously must have the skills to perform the work profitably and the willingness to do the job, I believe the fit must also be there from both the individual's and company's perspective. It's also important that a candidate recognize the importance of teamwork and bring with them high ethical and professional standards."*

QUESTION 29—YOUR EXPERIENCE REFLECTS SEVERAL MANAGEMENT POSITIONS. SINCE THIS IS NOT A MANAGEMENT POSITION, WILL THIS POSE A PROBLEM FOR YOU?

In these tough times, many job seekers are taking jobs for which they're clearly over qualified. In answering this question, you want to emphasize your strengths as they relate to the position you're applying for **and** where you feel you can contribute the most to the company. Don't give the hiring manager the impression that you're taking a lower position simply because you're out of work and need a paycheck.

Your response may be, *"I've enjoyed different roles throughout my career, several of which have been in management. This experience has helped me understand where my expertise and interests really lie. While this opportunity is not a managerial position, it does tie in with what I enjoy doing the most and, therefore, will enable me to maximize my contribution."*

QUESTION 30—WHAT DO YOU SEE AS THE MOST DIFFICULT TASK IN BEING A MANAGER?

Your answer will be different based on your own individual situation. During the interview, however, the hiring manager may discuss some of the challenges you'll be facing in this new position, so base your response on those management skills you have that relate to meeting those challenges.

A good general response may be: *"In my opinion, the toughest challenge for any manager is to recognize the diverse skills, personalities, and work ethic that each individual has, and be able to gain collaboration in building and maintaining a successful, positive team environment."*

QUESTION 31—WHAT DO YOUR SUBORDINATES THINK OF YOU?

It's important that when answering these questions, you be honest. While you may not have been personal friends with each of your subordinates, you, nevertheless, as a manager, were able to maintain a positive working relationship.

Your response may be, *"I'm confident that my subordinates have high regard for me as a manager. I'm sure that they would characterize me as someone who's ethical, has open communication, treats them fairly, and has been able to develop a good working relationship based on mutual respect and trust."*

QUESTION 32—HOW DO YOU MOTIVATE PEOPLE?

When answering this question, keep in mind that everyone is motivated differently and no one individual can motivate another. The best way to motivate someone is to create an environment that motivates them to act in a certain way.

It's important that you bring out this point in your response, which may be, *"I recognize that everyone is motivated differently. I don't believe any ONE person can motivate another to act in a particular way. However, I do believe that people are motivated by their environment. As a manager, I try to understand what motivates each of my team members and then create a positive environment that allows each of them to perform to their potential."*

QUESTION 33—HOW EFFECTIVE ARE YOU AT HANDLING MULTIPLE PROJECTS?

This can be a tricky question. On the one hand you don't want to create the impression that you're willing to take on an endless amount of additional work. On the other hand you want to make it clear that you're able to handle multiple tasks and meet project deadlines.

Your response may be: *"I'm committed to getting projects done on time and under budget. If I have the opportunity to take on additional project work that overlaps, I make sure I have the necessary resources to do the job. Otherwise I won't take on more than I can handle effectively."*

QUESTION 34—WHAT HAVE YOU LEARNED FROM THE JOBS YOU HAVE HELD?

A hiring manager asking this question doesn't want to hear how you've learned to be on time for work, never leave early or never eat lunch at your desk. On the contrary, they want to hear one or two things that you've learned from your past several jobs that have increased your value as an employee. Focus on your skills that are relevant to the position you're targeting. Remember they are hiring you for THEIR bottom line.

For example, if you're interviewing for a Senior Project Manager position, your response may be: *"In one of my prior positions I learned how to handle multiple projects at the same time. I also learned how to interact effectively with a diverse workforce made up of different personalities and work styles."*

Or, if you're interviewing for a Call Center Manager position, your response may be, *"Over the years, I've learned the importance of research in resolving a variety of challenging customer service issues, and I appreciate the value of exceptional customer service as it relates to company growth and profitability."*

CHAPTER FOURTEEN

Stress Questions

It's fair to say that if you're not prepared for the interview, any and all questions you may be asked can in fact be stressful. Even if you are fully prepared, there are some questions that may make you feel uncomfortable because they force you to talk about issues you'd rather not address. These types of questions can test your confidence and composure. Here are some examples:

QUESTION 35—YOUR RESUME SUGGESTS THAT YOU MAY BE OVERQUALIFIED OR TOO EXPERIENCED. DO YOU THINK THIS POSITION WILL BE TOO BORING FOR YOU?

This statement is often made during the interview when the hiring manager has a concern about your age, your willingness to do the job, or both. Your response should address the value you bring to the position with your maturity and experience and your interest in taking on positions of greater responsibility and challenge.

Your response may be: *"I don't believe I'm overqualified. More likely, I have the maturity and experience to step into this position and make an immediate contribution, without any kind of hand-holding or learning curve. That's a distinct benefit to you. This job is exactly what I want to do and I look at it as the first step to a long career with your company. My past experience means that I'll be in a position to take on more challenging responsibilities and therefore increase my value to you and the organization."*

QUESTION 36—WHAT COULD YOUR CURRENT EMPLOYER DO FOR YOU THAT WOULD PREVENT YOU FROM LOOKING FOR A JOB IN THE FIRST PLACE?

This question requires a careful answer that shows you're committed to exploring an alternative opportunity. Don't indicate any reason that would cause you to stay with your present employer. You want to assure the hiring manager you are serious about their job and not trying to play one company off against another!

Your response may be: *"There's really nothing that would change my decision to leave my present employer. I've made up my mind to explore other opportunities that will allow me to continue to grow professionally while maximizing my contribution to the best of my ability."*

QUESTION 37—YOU'VE HAD A NUMBER OF RECENT JOB CHANGES. WHAT COULD YOU TELL ME THAT WOULD MAKE ME BELIEVE THAT YOU WILL STAY WITH OUR COMPANY?

If you've left several jobs voluntarily, explain that your ability to grow professionally in each of those jobs had been hampered. If you left involuntarily, explain the circumstances, such as downsizing, a plant closing, or relocation of the company. Stress the fact that you're interested in joining the company for the long term. You'll have no reason to leave if you're challenged in your work, able to make a significant contribution, and compensated fairly for your efforts.

Your response may be: *"I've always looked at job opportunities from a long-term perspective; however, they haven't always been the right fit. As long as I'm able to make a significant contribution in a challenging work environment and fairly compensated for my efforts, I would have no reason to consider leaving."*

QUESTION 38—ARE YOU APPLYING FOR ANY OTHER JOBS?

If you've just begun your search and this is, in fact, the first company you've interviewed with, say so. Otherwise, state that you are currently exploring opportunities that will be the best fit for both you and the organization.

Your answer should refer to the position your interviewing for. For example, if you're applying for a Senior Project Manager position your response may be: *"While I have been looking at other opportunities, I'm excited about this particular position because it will allow me to apply my strong project management experience while learning new skills that will enhance my value to your company."*

QUESTION 39—WHY DID YOU STAY SO LONG AT YOUR LAST JOB?

If you joined the company in 1990 as a file clerk and you're still performing that same function 20 years later, this question could hurt you. On the other hand it can work in your favor if you can show a progression of increasingly responsible positions throughout the same period of time. Here you can demonstrate your long-term commitment to the company, regardless of the reason you left.

If you were downsized your response may be: *"I stayed with the company because I was enjoying a satisfying career and what I considered to be the ideal job."*

On the other hand, if you left voluntarily your response may be: *"While I was enjoying a long-term career with the company, recent changes affected the work environment to the point where I no longer was challenged and able to maximize my contribution."*

QUESTION 40—I'VE INTERVIEWED SEVERAL CANDIDATES, ALL WITH SIMILAR BACKGROUND AND EXPERIENCE TO YOURS. TELL ME, WHY SHOULD I HIRE YOU?

Remember, you're just one of several candidates competing for the job. If you respond by talking about how committed you are to your work, how dedicated and loyal you are, and how your skills and experience match the requirements of the job, etc., you're just reciting the same response your competitors will give. There's no differentiation. You're not giving the hiring manager a specific reason to hire YOU.

This is a great opportunity to use your Management Endorsements (see Chapter Two in this book and TheHireRoad™ system at www.TheHireChallenge.com for more information on this powerful and unique tool).

With this tool, you'll be able to separate yourself head and shoulders from your competition with this suggested response: *"I'm sure whoever you choose for this position must bring with them a track record of exceptional performance. Wouldn't you agree? I have the ability to deliver. I've done it for former employers and I can do it for you. Let me show you what some of my former managers have said about MY performance..."*

QUESTION 41—THERE APPEAR TO BE GAPS BETWEEN EMPLOYMENT ON YOUR RESUME. WHAT WERE YOU DOING DURING THOSE TIMES?

Answering this question will be different for everybody. I would suggest being proactive and addressing the gaps in your employment first, before the hiring manager asks the question.

Just remember to stay positive about the reason for the gaps. Don't be defensive. You may have had a family situation that required your attention for a period of time. Or you may have been actively involved in a job search during which you took the time to carefully consider your next career move. Or you may have gone back to school to upgrade your skills and therefore enhance your value. When answering this question, avoid saying something like, *"I just decided to take some time off before going back to work."*

CHAPTER FIFTEEN

Salary Questions

Salary questions often come up in the interview process even though salary negotiation should only begin once you've been selected as the candidate of choice or,
at the very least, are on a short list. You may be asked about your salary history
or desired salary during the preliminary screening process or when filling out an
application. Or you may be asked during the face-to-face interview.

Just remember, the subject of compensation should **always** be raised by the
hiring manager, not you. Here are some typical salary related questions you can
expect:

QUESTION 42—WHAT SALARY ARE YOU LOOKING FOR?

Regardless of when this question is asked during the interview process, don't
name a specific number. If really pressed, give a range.

If this question is asked at the beginning of the interview, your response should
be something like, *"At this point in our discussion, I don't have enough information
about the requirements of the position and how my skills and abilities can meet your
specific needs. I'm sure toward the end of our meeting I'll be in a better position to
discuss compensation."*

If this question is asked at the end of the interview, your response would be
something like, *"Well, based on our discussion today, I think it's clear that this
position is a great fit for me professionally and for your organization. I'm sure
whatever offer you'd make to me would be very fair."*

QUESTION 43—WHAT IS YOUR CURRENT SALARY?

The subject of salary should never come up for discussion until the hiring
manager has selected you as the candidate of choice or included you on a very
short list. However, you may be asked this question at any time during the interview
process. If you've provided a specific number or range when filling out the job
application, you need to be consistent when answering this question during the
face-to-face interview.

If you omitted this information on the application, you'll want to ask the hiring manager if you can compare the responsibilities of your current or previous position with those of the position you're interviewing for. That way you'll both be able to see if the positions are compatible with respect to salary. If you do provide your salary information, give a range instead of a specific number. Keep in mind your worth to your current or former employer will be different than the worth you offer this new company.

A suggested response could be: *"My current compensation is in the range of $70K to $80K. However, I'm more interested in discussing the value I can bring to your company with respect to this particular position. Can we compare my current responsibilities with those I would have in this job? That way we can see if the positions are compatible with respect to salary."*

QUESTION 44—DUE TO YOUR INEXPERIENCE, WOULD YOU BE WILLING TO CONSIDER THIS POSITION AT A LOWER SALARY?

This is a catch-22 question. First I would ask what salary range is being offered. This lower salary may not be financially viable for you so therefore this opportunity may not be practical. On the other hand, if the lower salary is acceptable to you, your response should focus on your opportunity to grow with the company rather than immediate compensation. By learning additional skills and taking on more responsibilities, your value to the company will increase along with your compensation.

Your response could be, *"I'm more interested in the opportunity to join your company rather than immediate compensation. I'm confident that, by learning new skills and taking on more responsibilities, my compensation will, over time, reflect my added value to your company."*

CHAPTER SIXTEEN

Questions YOU Need to Ask

One major way to differentiate yourself from other candidates, most of whom will tend to be passive and wait to be asked, is to ask questions of your own. In addition, asking questions may have the hiring manager take over the conversation and minimize the number of hard questions you would otherwise have been asked.

Being proactive during the interview and asking relevant questions will not only help differentiate you from your competition, but will also provide you with useful information concerning the position, the company, and the work environment. Listen carefully to the answers, take notes, and take advantage of any opportunity to highlight your strengths, and reinforce positive feedback you receive from the hiring manager.

In addition to several questions about the company in general, and several more about the job itself, you'll want to consider asking the following questions:

QUESTION 45—WHAT BROUGHT YOU HERE TO XYZ COMPANY AND WHAT KEEPS YOU HERE?

This is a great opportunity for you to establish the chemistry that's so critical to a successful interview. By asking this question at the outset of the interview, you're showing personal interest in the hiring manager, allowing them to talk about themselves. Hopefully the response you'll receive will provide you the opportunity to reinforce your interest in the position and the company.

QUESTION 46—WHY IS THIS POSITION OPEN? AND HOW LONG HAS IT BEEN OPEN?

The response you receive to this question can reveal some red flags about the position. Depending on how long the position has been open, you may or may not want to ask why it has not yet been filled and how many candidates they've interviewed so far. If the position has been open for a long time and they've interviewed many candidates, the response could indicate various drawbacks, such as salary, responsibilities, location, management style, work environment, etc.

QUESTION 47—WHAT DO YOU CONSIDER TO BE THE TOP DUTIES OF THIS POSITION?

This is an important question because the answer may reveal characteristics of the job that are different from your initial interpretation. You'll learn firsthand the concerns and true needs of the hiring manager, while the job description may have only provided a cursory overview.

QUESTION 48—WHAT WOULD YOU HOPE TO ACCOMPLISH BY HIRING ME?

This is a great question that encourages the hiring manager to discuss the problems and issues at hand. It gives you the perfect opportunity to demonstrate how your skills, experience, expertise, and style can successfully address those challenges.

QUESTION 49—WHAT CAN YOU TELL ME ABOUT THE PEOPLE I WOULD BE WORKING WITH?

This question can help you understand the environment in which you'll be working and the company's emphasis on teamwork. It gives you the opportunity to stress just how important teamwork is to your success and the success of those you'll be interacting with.

QUESTION 50—HOW DO YOU, OR HOW WILL YOU, DETERMINE A SUCCESSFUL CANDIDATE FOR THIS POSITION?

The response you get to this question will enable you to key in on the specific characteristics the manager is looking for in a successful candidate. It allows you to reinforce how your skills, experience, expertise, and style characterize what he or she is looking for.

QUESTION 51—HOW WOULD MY PERFORMANCE BE MEASURED FOR THE FIRST 30, 60, AND 90 DAYS OF EMPLOYMENT?

This is an important question to ask. You certainly want to know what the hiring manager's expectations are of your performance during the first several months of employment.

QUESTION 52—BASED ON OUR DISCUSSION TODAY, IS THERE ANYTHING IN MY BACKGROUND THAT WOULD PREVENT ME FROM BEING CONSIDERED THE TOP CANDIDATE FOR THIS POSITION?

This is a critical question to ask because it forces the hiring manager to reveal any concerns he or she may have about your candidacy for the job. By asking this question toward the end of the interview, you're able to address and hopefully resolve those concerns FACE-TO-FACE. You don't want to find out days later that you were passed over due to some lack of experience or skill. When that happens, it's what I call the Post-Interview-Traumatic-Syndrome (P.I.T.S.). Asking this question at the appropriate time in the interview will help you avoid the P.I.T.S.

BONUS QUESTION:

THIS POSITION IS A GREAT FIT FOR ME PROFESSIONALLY AND FOR YOUR ORGANIZATION. I CAN DO THIS JOB WELL AND I CAN DO IT FOR YOU PROFITABLY. I HAVE JUST ONE FINAL QUESTION. HOW SOON WOULD YOU NEED ME TO START?

If you've determined during the interview that you want the position, this is **THE** most important question to ask. Regardless of the response you receive, this closing question demonstrates your initiative and tells the hiring manager that you want the job.

Asking this question will trigger a commitment to a plan of action. In other words, what are the next steps in the process? It's highly unlikely that the hiring manager will respond to your question by saying "How about 9 a.m. tomorrow morning?" The response given, however, should indicate what those next steps are. When the interview is over and you're shaking hands, don't say something like *"I enjoyed meeting with you to discuss this position, and I look forward to hearing from you soon."* Continue to separate yourself from your competition by asking for the job!

CHAPTER SEVENTEEN

Summary and Closing

I've discussed a cross section of some of the most common questions you can expect to be asked in an interview. Some you may find easy to respond to, while others can be more challenging and will require some preparation.

As you think about your upcoming interview be prepared to answer a tough "on the spot" question that requires you to answer with a specific demonstration of your skills.

Here's an example: If you're in sales, you may be asked in the interview if you consider yourself to be a good salesperson. Your obvious response of "yes" may well be followed up with a request to give an example, such as "OK, sell me this stapler!"

In this situation you would proceed by asking questions to identify the customer's needs. After identifying the needs, you would then point out the features, advantages, and benefits that meet those needs. Then you would identify any concerns or objections that may hinder the decision to buy. After resolving those concerns, you would attempt to close the sale by asking what color they would like and what is their preferred delivery date.

When you're out there in the job market, YOU are the product and YOU are the salesperson. As taught in the Product Demonstration milestone of TheHireRoad™, your approach in selling yourself as the preferred solution is exactly the same as selling the stapler.

Another example would be an "on the spot" project question. If you are a Marketing Manager or a Graphic Designer, you may be asked to describe how you would complete a specific project, such as the creation of a marketing brochure or the marketing of a new product in retail stores around the U.S. Here you would talk about the various skills that have enabled you to consistently bring projects in on time and under budget. These would include needs analysis, resource allocation, project milestones, budgeting, collaboration and effective team leadership.

Think about possible "on the spot" questions, that can be asked that tie in specifically with your expertise. Hiring managers want people who can think on their feet and can respond on the spur of the moment.

Anticipate questions and *practice* your responses ahead of time so you don't get caught off guard.

SECTION 4

Negotiating Your True Worth!

CHAPTER EIGHTEEN

They Made You a Job Offer!

YOU GOT AN OFFER!

Well-deserved congratulations! All of your efforts have paid off. You've completed the interview process, become the preferred solution, and now the company wants to enter into a relationship with you. You will have received either a written or verbal job offer and the delicate dance between you as the job seeker and your potential employer over what you will be paid really begins.

Many job search systems and guidebooks leave this chapter out because talking about money after all the time and effort it took to get your job seems anti-climactic. After all, you wanted a job and now you have one. You should be able to trust the employer to make a fair offer right?

Wrong!

This is the most critical step in establishing your true worth to the company. How you position yourself now, at the beginning of your relationship, will continue throughout your career with this company! You want to receive a package that is fair, reasonable, and reflects your worth to the company. Your employer on the other hand, wants to get you for as low a cost as they reasonably can without insulting you.

The offer will usually contain a title or level, an outline of your total compensation package, starting date, and location. But there may be a big difference between what they're offering and what you're worth. It is your job to ensure your price and their offer reflects your true worth to the organization.

Obviously, if the offer meets or exceeds your expectations, you should consider accepting it as presented. However, if the offer falls short of meeting your expectations, you need to negotiate.

If you've been out of work for some time, you're obviously going to be feeling a great sense of relief. It can be very tempting to accept the offer as is and start the job right away. But keep in mind, there's a strong possibility that you can negotiate a better compensation package, depending on your leverage.

As you carefully assess the various components of your job offer, understand that almost every one of these components can be negotiated! Few companies extend offers that are accepted at face value, and negotiation is expected. Not negotiating can actually be a negative sign to a new employer.

The information that follows will help you understand how to assess your needs and requirements, determine your worth, evaluate the offer, and then negotiate for more.

ACKNOWLEDGING YOUR OFFER

It is customary for the hiring manager to verbally extend an offer to you. Sometimes it will happen at the close of the interview (or the final interview if you've had more than one). Sometimes it will be a telephone call a few days after the interview. Depending on the position, the offer may come from the hiring manager, your new manager-to-be, or from human resources.

If you get a verbal offer make sure you understand the job title, job responsibilities, salary, start date, and benefits. Then ask for the offer in writing.

It is not a job offer until it is in writing. Kinda' like "it ain't pay day until the check cashes."

After you've received the written offer, contact the hiring manager immediately and express your thanks for the written offer. Then ask for at least one or two days to evaluate it before giving your acceptance. Make sure you ask if there is a deadline for your decision. Some offers will include expiration dates, especially if there is a pressing need or project deadline associated with the position.

You can send a formal acceptance letter or a simple thank-you, depending on the offer and your planned response. If you want time to negotiate, the thank-you note and a request for a few days to review and consider the offer is perfect—classy and professional.

If you're entertaining offers from several different companies, you may want to ask for even more time. However, never take longer than the hiring manager is willing to provide. There is a thin line between a reasonable time to consider an offer and appearing indecisive.

It's gratifying to know that at this point in the entire process **you** now have the tactical advantage! You have the high ground and the most **power**. The company has decided they want **you**. They have invested their time and energy in selecting you, so based on this leverage, take advantage and negotiate the best possible package.

JOB TYPES

In today's economy there are several job categories, including temporary, holiday, contract, and part-time, being offered to job seekers. But our focus is job offers for full-time positions.

Note that there are two types of full-time employees—hourly and salaried. Hourly is usually a lower income, less responsible position. You are literally paid for the hours you work and have to punch in and punch out on a clock or computer. There are usually strict state or local rules on overtime, breaks, and benefits. Hourly wages are set by the state as minimum wage or by a contract through a union or other group. Benefits and perks are limited. This means there is generally little to no flexibility on the part of the employer.

The other paid position is called salaried. Salaried employees are not on the clock and while you may have regular hours from 8 a.m. to 5 p.m., you are expected to work as long as a job takes. There may be regular breaks and/or lunch hours but if you work through them or work an occasional 60-hour week, there is no additional salary. Management or other professional jobs are usually salaried positions.

Both types of full-time positions can benefit from using TheHireAdvantage™ milestones in Packaging, Promotion, and Product Demonstration. However, Pricing is usually not applicable to hourly employees. So the balance of this book will focus on salaried employees because employers can be more flexible and negotiations are more likely.

OFFER COMPONENTS

Generally speaking your job offer will outline the salary, location, job title, and responsibilities. It may be specific on benefits or use a throw-away line like "standard employee benefits." If appropriate, there may be incentives or special bonuses.

Make sure you understand **exactly** what components are included in traditional offers for the position and the location. If you don't know, ask people in similar jobs. Use your network or ask in forums like LinkedIn. Knowledge is power and, in this case, money in your pocket.

Most jobs (and your sense of value) are determined by your salary. Well before you have your first interview, do your salary research! Gather outside information on the current market value of your position. Credible Internet resources for this information include Salary.com, Payscale.com, Jobstar.org, and Indeed.com. Their tools should give you a good market rate for the salary of peers in your position in your local area. Salary is obviously the most important piece of your job offer but it is **not** the only part!

Don't overlook important items, such as bonuses, commissions, expenses for moving, etc., that put cash in your pocket. But don't be distracted by visions of huge commission or bonus checks. Always start with the **known** base salary.

Keep in mind that key components found in most job offers vary from one company to the next. Depending on the job and the industry there may be other components, such as a uniform allowance or child care. These other components could have a major impact on your decision to accept or reject the offer. Take health coverage, for example, where the scope of coverage will vary extensively between employers. While that may not be important to a healthy 20-something college graduate, it may be critical to a family with children.

You should also be aware of the specific job responsibilities, the reporting structure, vacation time, how you'll be paid, your start date, and your hours. Evaluate these components carefully to make sure they fall in line with your requirements.

It's essential that you understand all the benefits you'll receive, as well as company policies and procedures. If not included with your written offer, call the HR department and ask for a written explanation of benefits and an employee handbook. The larger the company, the more likely it is that benefits will be standardized for employees at various levels.

It is imperative that you create a checklist and evaluate every component of your offer. As you create your checklist you'll see there are quite a number of items that you can negotiate as part of your overall total compensation package. It's important that you review this list carefully, identifying those components that you want included in your offer. When considering your offer letter, you really need to think about your value to the employer.

YOUR WORTH IN THE MARKETPLACE

Worth versus price is an ongoing discussion for job seekers. You are only worth what the other person thinks you are worth! That means worth is in the eye of the beholder or, in this case, your employer! Sadly, your value or worth to an employer may be quite different than what you actually perceive your worth to be. This fact is especially hard for experienced employees entering new positions or new industries.

The value or worth of an employee is largely based on supply and demand. If you are in the pool with a lot of job applicants with similar skills and experience, you may have become a commodity. Being a commodity means you look like everyone else and are replaceable with just about any other candidate. Commodities are generally purchased cheaply.

However, most companies are usually willing to pay market price for a position if the job seeker is worth the investment. So it becomes critical that you know what that market price is and how to position and sell yourself for the highest possible value. How do you find out your worth in the marketplace?

Basically, you have to research competitive salary ranges and benefits for similar positions in the same industry in the same geography while keeping in mind the supply and demand for your particular skills. If accepting the offer means relocating to another area, don't forget to take into consideration the cost-of-living differential since this will most certainly impact your walk-away point. There are a number of resources online to help you determine your worth in the marketplace, including:

    www.Payscale.com
    www.JobSearchIntelligence.com
    www.SalaryCalculator.com
    www.Salary.com
    http://calculator.GIJobs.com

I would also go to www.BankRate.com to get a good comparison for cost of living differentials based on geographic location.

Typically, there's a big difference between what a company is willing to pay you, what you can reasonably expect, and what you'd like to be paid. There is nothing sinister or evil in this reality. Whenever we plan on making a purchase, such as a new car, refrigerator, TV, or stereo, we always want to get the best product at the lowest price. We want to get the best deal.

A company is no exception. Employers want to invest as little as possible to solve their problems. That means buying equipment and hiring employees for as little as they can, yet retaining the best value and talent. Corporations with stockholders actually have a legal fiduciary responsibility to try to acquire your services at the lowest possible investment!

While you may perceive yourself as a legend in your own mind, and therefore the greatest thing since sliced bread, the package you're offered may be lower than what you're expecting. This happens because the company would obviously like to acquire your talent at the lowest price. Your best defense is to do the research necessary to know your true worth.

For example, the company may have internally established a salary range of $65,000 to $85,000 a year with a moving bonus if asked. But they've made you an opening offer of $70,000 a year and no bonuses. However, your research shows you should reasonably expect at least $80,000 based on your experience and expect a relocation bonus. Sharing your research will help you negotiate a better offer. This is why knowing the position's worth in the marketplace ahead of time is so critical.

CHAPTER NINETEEN

Key Considerations

BE PREPARED

To be successful in negotiation, you must thoroughly prepare for that negotiation. This begins by determining your key considerations. These are the components that you've identified ahead of time as **must-haves** in a job offer. Once these are identified, the next step is to compare your key considerations to the major components of your offer. This will help you identify those issues to be negotiated.

Your ability to successfully negotiate key considerations requires research and background information. Having that knowledge can mean the difference between accepting and rejecting an offer. And you do not want to accept or reject an offer based on assumptions and lack of data!

KEY CONSIDERATIONS

It's essential to know your key considerations before evaluating an offer. Your key considerations are your must-haves. These are things you consider as critical in any offer and are unique to you. However, most include items such as base salary, incentive programs, health insurance, retirement plan, minimum vacation, relocation expenses, company car or car allowance, etc. You need to make a list based on your research and expectations.

It's also important that you understand all the additional benefits you'll receive, as well as company policies and procedures. If these are not included with your written offer, call the HR department and ask for a written explanation of benefits and an employee handbook.

CASH COMPENSATION

Now let's focus on what is usually the most important key consideration which is money. It's almost always at the top of the must-have list, and rightly so. While the total package may contain other attractive components, your offer obviously has to be financially viable for you to even consider it. Cash compensation typically includes a base salary and some form of incentive pay, such as bonuses or commission. Only the base salary should be defined as a key consideration, since this represents the fixed amount of income you'll be receiving, as compared to a bonus or commission, which is variable. Start with this number because everything else will likely be outside your employer's control. For example, you cannot count on commissions or bonuses because you do not control the client's sales decision. And remember, a bonus is not a guarantee. Many companies discontinue or just provide the minimum bonuses during rough times. In addition, the IRS takes about 30 percent of that bonus prior to the physical payout. I'd rather have a bigger paycheck than a possible bonus.

You need to determine the absolute minimum base salary required to meet your everyday obligations. If you haven't already determined what this number should be, your first homework assignment will be to carefully assess your financial needs to arrive at what I call your **walk-away number.**

How do you determine your walk-away number? Look at all your monthly bills and figure out what amount is needed to meet those obligations. Remember to use after-tax figures and don't forget to factor in your spouse's fixed income, if any. Use the sample *Financial Analysis Worksheet* in the Summary and Conclusion to help you assess your walk-away number.

This exercise will provide you with a number that represents the absolute minimum you need to earn as a base salary. This then becomes your walk-away number. Do not include commissions, bonuses, or other anticipated income that you can't count on.

Even though there may be variables that surface during negotiation that may impact your walk-away number, knowing this number ahead of time will help you determine if the final offer is financially viable.

Unfortunately, many people in transition fail to go through this exercise, and, because they've been out of work for some time, they become desperate and accept a position where the salary is insufficient to meet their needs. They discover this several weeks into their new job, become financially stressed, and begin to think about looking for a higher-paying job. This is **not** what you want to do.

What if a job offer has been made and, even after negotiation, the most the employer will offer is still less than your bottom-line (no-go) number? What should you do to ensure you are making the right decision?

Stick to your base salary number!

The whole reason to know your walk-away number is to help you make the right decision. You won't have to stress over accepting the offer. If you don't hit your salary goal, you agree to part ways. You say, "I'm really sorry we weren't able to make it work, but I'm going to have to pass."

Did that scare you?

What if you have been out of work for months and this is the first sure-thing you've gotten? Shouldn't you take it and work really, really hard to get a raise?

This is a recipe for disaster. You will be starting a new job knowing you settled for less than you are worth. You will likely become resentful and an unhappy employee. Also, the employer has now established that you can be bought cheaply. They are not likely to respect you or worry about you leaving in the future.

MUST-HAVES

Once you've established your walk-away number, your next homework assignment is to identify any remaining key considerations, or **must-haves.** Remember, these will influence your decision to accept or reject the offer. Don't skip this step or take it lightly. I have seen job seekers take jobs based on the salary alone only to become disenchanted and even lose money because they neglected these other items!

Typical must-haves may include:

- Work schedule (days, evenings, shift work, extensive overtime without compensation)
- Commute time
- Business travel
- Health care benefits and percentage share
- Vacation
- Education benefits
- Retirement plans (401K, stock plan, pension, etc.)
- Moving bonus or housing allowance (important if you are moving from a low-cost area in the Midwest to an area with a high cost of living, like Los Angeles or New York City)
- Working environment (indoors, outdoors, high risk)
- Lifestyle friendliness (domestic partner benefits, etc.)

- Tenure, work guarantees

- Advancement potential

- Others that may be unique to you

You might find that, although the majority of your requirements are met, there may be certain aspects that make the offer unacceptable. These could include the **red flags** you identified during the interview process, such as extensive travel or a potential merger that may adversely affect your position. Just like the walk-away salary number, determine if there are any walk-away must-haves.

Make the list as complete as you can. This will help ensure you don't regret it later.

COMPANY LIFE CYCLE

Once you've identified your own personal key considerations and established your walk-away number, look at the company's life cycle.

All companies go through several stages in their lifespan. They begin as start-ups, enter growth periods, and, if lucky, become stable. As we've seen in the current economy, they can also be struggling or in decline. Where they are and how long they expect to be there will directly impact many of the major components of your job offer. Therefore, knowing this will help you understand your worth in the marketplace and interpret their offer more rationally and allow you to negotiate more effectively.

If you're considering joining a start-up company, you can expect the salary to be low, the incentives like stock ownership to be high, the benefits to be low to none, and the perks to be low. You should also expect there will be no stability or long-term employment potential until the company has survived at least five years.

On the other hand, if the company is in a growth mode, the salary, incentives, benefits, and perks will usually be competitive. If the company is well established, you can typically expect a higher salary, low incentives and benefits, and higher perks, as well as the potential for longer-term employment.

Look at the media on the company. Google them and see if there are rumors of takeovers or imminent bankruptcy. Are they publicly traded or privately held? Are they family owned and what is the position of any children? If you want to be promoted and there are family members in the organization, there could easily be family politics. These are all red flags.

WHAT'S YOUR PRICE?

You've done your homework. You've established your walk-away number, identified your key considerations, and determined your worth (salary and other benefits) in the marketplace through research. Now it's time to evaluate the offer, or the price the company is willing to pay for your talent.

You now have to determine if the price (the total package) the potential employer is offering is an accurate reflection of your worth for the position. Remember that while the hiring manager may be excited about your potential contribution to the company, you are still an expense item on his or her budget. One of management's responsibilities is to control costs. Therefore, the offer they make may be at the low end of the range for the position to help the bottom line. This is where negotiation comes in, the objective being to resolve differences through give-and-take, thereby reaching a middle ground.

You'll most likely have to come down in your expectations while the company will have to come up to meet them. You must assume the company will try to acquire your talent for the lowest price possible. Therefore, be fully prepared to negotiate what you feel is your true worth, considering all components of your offer. If the compensation package does not have deal breakers, but still does not meet your expectations, then it's time to negotiate.

CHAPTER TWENTY

The Art of Negotiation

BASIS FOR NEGOTIATION

Your leverage in the negotiation process will depend on how much your skills are needed by the company.

If the skills you bring to the table are in short supply, your leverage may be strong. On the other hand if your skills are in plentiful supply (e.g., you are a commodity), you may have very little leverage, so be careful.

As I outlined in the prior chapters, do the research necessary to know your worth in the marketplace and the price the potential employer should pay for the location and tasks. This is the basis and starting point as you begin negotiations.

THE PROCESS OF NEGOTIATION

So what is negotiation? In simple terms, it's the resolution of differences through discussion and collaboration. It involves working together to explore each other's expectations with the objective of finding mutually acceptable ways to satisfy them. The key words here are mutually acceptable. You want the proverbial win-win scenario where each party feels good about some part of the eventual deal.

Negotiation is **not** an exercise where there's one winner and one loser. While it's natural to feel some anxiety, enter into the process of negotiation with a positive attitude. Use your power of influence to reach the goal of establishing a win-win situation.

One important thing to remember! You'll most likely be negotiating with your future boss. This will hopefully be a long-term relationship, so try to avoid any situation that may negatively affect it. Be professional and firm but not rude or demanding.

Buying Signals

Initial negotiation may have begun during the interview when you started receiving buying signals from the hiring manager. Such signals indicate that you're seriously being considered as the preferred solution. For example, the hiring manager may have begun selling you on the benefits of working for the company and initiated a discussion about compensation, or the conversation became more about problem-solving as if you were already employed by the company. Another signal is the interview may have run much longer than scheduled or the hiring manager introduced you to others with whom you were not originally scheduled to meet. These are all positive buying signals.

If the hiring manager **has** decided that you're the best fit for the position, he or she may initiate a discussion concerning certain terms of your compensation package on the spot. When this occurs, regardless of what you negotiate and agree to during the interview process, **always** make sure it's reflected in your written offer.

Pros and Cons of Your Offer

Having received the written offer, you need to look carefully at all the **pros** and **cons** associated with this position. Use the sample *Job Offer Component Checklist* in the Summary and Conclusion of this book to help you prepare for effective negotiation and enable you to objectively determine whether or not to accept the final offer.

The *Job Offer Component Checklist* is by no means complete or customized to your unique situation and needs. There may be many other pros and cons associated with your and your family's position that need to be considered. So be sure to list as many positive and negative aspects of this position as you can.

Deal Breakers

When making your pro-and-con list, be sure to include any conditions or potential job attributes that would make it impossible for you to say "yes" to the job. These are known as deal breakers. And again, these are unique to you and to your family situation. One applicant's deal breaker may be another applicant's throw-away item.

Deal breakers are just that, facets of the job that simply cannot be negotiated away. For example, if you are a single parent with young children, a position with extensive overnight travel or long commutes would not only be a con, it could be a potential deal breaker.

Legitimate Issues to Negotiate

After you've identified your pros and cons, look at the list of "cons" and identify those that are legitimate and reasonable to negotiate. Salary and benefits are usually legitimate issues to negotiate. Another may be excessive travel or the necessity to work long hours, which are common in start-up companies.

Check to see which items are flexible with your potential employer and which are iron-clad and in concrete. Asking if they may be flexible is the first step in negotiation and, depending on the answer, may turn a con into a deal breaker.

Throw-Away Items

Now look again at the cons and see which could be *throw-away items* in the negotiation. These are the items you'd like to negotiate more in your favor. However, your inability to do so will not affect your decision to accept the offer. You put them on the table to see if you can improve them but would not walk away if they remain as originally offered.

A good example of a throw-away item would be vacation. Let's say you've been accustomed to four weeks vacation per year and your potential employer is offering two. You may ask for three, or even four, but if you don't get the additional weeks it won't affect your decision to accept the offer.

Another example is a signing bonus. In today's economy these are rare and often considered a throw-away item unless it happens to be a standard in the industry or you happen to have an exceptional or rare skill.

STRATEGIES TO NEGOTIATE A HIGHER BASE SALARY

There's no need to approach the subject of base salary if you've negotiated an acceptable number during the interview process, or if the offer includes a number above what you expected. However, if you need to negotiate, there are several strategies that may get you a higher base salary:

Strategy #1

Make sure the salary you're offered is reflective of the industry standards that you researched prior to the interview. If not, let the hiring manager know that you've done your research and the offer falls short of what is reasonable.

When negotiating salary, the old saying applies: "Whoever names a number first loses." Therefore, let the hiring manager name a specific number first. If that number is not in line with industry standards, and there's no adjustment made, you may need to rethink your intention of accepting the offer. Remember, companies should pay market value for your skills.

Assuming the salary is within the acceptable range for the industry, but lower than expected, your first strategy is to ask the manager if there's any **wiggle room** to that base salary number. This is a warm and fuzzy way of saying you'd like to see the amount raised.

Don't suggest a specific dollar amount of increase, but rather let the hiring manager come back to you with a revised number. If you're comfortable with this number, express your agreement and move on to the next issue to be negotiated. If not, try the second strategy.

Strategy #2

Try to negotiate a **salary increase based on short-term job performance.** The majority of companies grant salary increases based on the outcome of yearly performance reviews. The strategy here is to negotiate a six-month, or even three-month review rather than waiting for the end of your first full year of employment. Ask for the opportunity to demonstrate just how well you can perform in your new job with the understanding that you'll both sit down in three or six months and review that performance. This can be a win-win situation because it puts the onus on you to deliver, and the manager is only agreeing to a review, not necessarily guaranteeing you a raise. A favorable review, however, will more than likely result in a bump in your base salary.

If there's no wiggle room, and the hiring manager has been reluctant to give you an early review, it's time to move on to the third strategy.

Strategy #3

Ask for a **reconfiguration of your job responsibilities.** In other words, ask for more responsibilities to be added to the position to justify a higher salary. This increases your value and should warrant a salary that meets your acceptable number. Very few candidates ask for additional responsibilities when negotiating an offer.

Despite your efforts at skillful negotiation, you may find that the hiring manager is unwilling or unable to increase the amount of base salary. He or she is also unwilling or unable to grant a short-term performance review, and there is no way the job responsibilities can be reconfigured. If this is the case there is one last strategy to try.

Strategy #4

Regardless of outcome, you may want to try to negotiate one of your throw-away items, such as a **sign-on bonus or modified commission plan,** as a means of increasing your first-year total compensation. A signing bonus is a one-time expense for the company and is not recurring. Again, don't name a number first. Let the hiring manager come back to you with a number.

THE NEGOTIATION DISCUSSION

So who does the negotiating? If you've been working with a search firm, let the recruiter do the negotiating. Make sure he or she understands ahead of time what your key considerations, requirements, and concerns are so the recruiter can effectively negotiate on your behalf. Be sure to let them know about any deal breakers!

If no search firm is involved, call the hiring manager directly and ask for a meeting to discuss certain terms of the offer. The ideal situation is to meet face-to-face; however, if that's not possible you can negotiate over the phone.

Avoid negotiating with human resources! They will be the enforcers of policy and history. It is also highly unlikely that they will be able to assess your worth in the position. They will have little to no decision-making authority. Generally speaking only the hiring manager can do that. Be respectful, but remember HR sometimes stands for "hiring resistance."

Begin your discussion by mentioning the **areas of agreement** in the offer. Easy ones will likely be location and job activities. Then transition into the specific items of concern to you, such as salary and benefits. Here's where your list of deal killers and throw-away items comes into play.

CHAPTER TWENTY-ONE

Summary and Conclusion

Once you receive the final, revised offer, take a step back and take one last look at your list of **pros** and **cons**. Then decide if this is truly the right opportunity for you.

Successful negotiation occurs when both parties are able to understand and resolve their respective differences in a reasonable way. Your attitude and demeanor will go a long way in achieving that goal. Always begin negotiation by expressing your desire to reach an equitable agreement.

Remember, even during negotiation you need to continue to **focus on the value** you bring to the organization. Emphasize how your performance will **impact profitability.** This is the **only** reason they want to hire you.

You've negotiated your compensation package, received the revised offer in writing, reviewed your final list of pros and cons, and now you're ready to begin your new job. The last step is to **confirm your acceptance, both verbally and in a letter to the hiring manager.**

And with that **congratulations.** You are now well on your way to being one of the lucky employed!

Welcome to "The HIRED Road!" You should now know what you are worth for the jobs you have sought and understand how to evaluate and negotiate to receive a fair price from your employer.

I hope I have freed you from the C.R.A.P. and have shown you how to avoid becoming a commodity in the job market and how to successfully use the interview to demonstrate your value. With the information in this section you should be able to negotiate the offer you both need and want.

I hope you have learned valuable skills that will ensure your successful transition now and when you need it in the future.

However, if you feel you need additional help and coaching in any of the four milestones, I humbly suggest you investigate the proven job search system TheHireRoad™, by visiting the website www.TheHireChallenge.com

Also, please feel free to contact me at TheHireChallenge™ website with questions and suggestions for future books and articles.

FINANCIAL ANALYSIS WORKSHEET

You've had the interview! You've been offered a position! Now you must decide whether the salary offered meets your financial needs. This worksheet will help you efficiently compare your monthly expenses with your projected monthly net income. If your net income is higher than your monthly expenses, you can feel comfortable with the salary offered. However, if your expenses are higher than your income, it may be time to negotiate your salary.

Monthly Ongoing Expenses

Itemize costs that are ongoing each month

Mortgage (including monthly property taxes) _____

Rent (in lieu of mortgage OR in new location) _____

Association fees(s) _____

Utilities (gas, electric, water) _____

Telephone _____

Cable/Internet _____

Car payments _____

Insurance:

    Health _____

    Car _____

    Homeowner _____

    Life _____

Child care/nanny _____

Housekeeper/gardner _____

Other unique to you _____

ADD EVERYTHING TOGETHER FOR TOTAL
MONTHLY ONGOING EXPENSES

TOTAL_____ **(A)**

Monthly Variable Expenses

This list is for those items you spend money on occasionally. These are things you could cut down, if necessary. Do this **twice**—once for your current expenses and once for your anticipated or revised budget with your new job. You are looking for opportunities to change your lifestyle to take a job that may have a lower salary.

Current Budget

Clothing

    Purchases   _____

    Dry cleaning   _____

    Tailoring   _____

Food

    Groceries   _____

    Dining out   _____

    Fast food   _____

Transportation costs

    Gas   _____

    Repairs (including oil changes)   _____

    Car wash/wax   _____

    Parking costs   _____

    Public transportation   _____

Leisure activities

    Vacations/trips   _____

    Movies/Plays/Concerts   _____

    Subscriptions   _____

    Golf/Games   _____

Gifts   _____

Education

    College tuition   _____

    Extension classes   _____

    Books/supplies   _____

Charitable contributions   _____

Other   _____

        TOTAL _____**(B)**

Revised Budget

Clothing

    Purchases   _____

    Dry cleaning   _____

    Tailoring   _____

Food

    Groceries   _____

    Dining out   _____

    Fast food   _____

Transportation costs

    Gas   _____

    Repairs (incuding oil changes)   _____

    Car wash/wax   _____

    Parking costs   _____

    Public transportation   _____

Leisure activities

    Vacations/trips   _____

    Movies/plays/concerts   _____

    Subscriptions   _____

    Golf/games   _____

Gifts   _____

Education

    College tuition   _____

    Extension classes   _____

    Books/supplies   _____

Charitable contributions   _____

Other   _____

TOTAL _____ **(C)**

Monthly Estimated Net Income

List all your sources of established and consistent monthly income (after taxes)

Proposed salary/wages

Commissions (average)

Bonuses (average)

Unemployment insurance

Severance pay

Alimony/child support

Investment interest

Rental property

Home-based business

Spouse salary

Other

TOTAL MONTHLY NET INCOME _____ **(D)**

Monthly Budget Summary

Subtracting your total Monthly Ongoing Expenses and Monthly Variable Expenses from your Total Estimated Monthly Net Income will help you determine if you need to negotiate the salary offered for your new position.

TOTAL MONTHLY NET INCOME (D)   _____

                                                Minus (-)

TOTAL MONTHLY ONGOING EXPENSES (A)   _____

                                                Minus (-)

TOTAL MONTHLY VARIABLE
EXPENSES (B) or (C)   _____

                                                Equals (=)

NET MONTHLY DIFFERENCE   _____

After subtracting your monthly expenses from your net income, if the net monthly difference has money to spare, the offer is probably acceptable. However, if there is no spare money or the amount is not enough for you, you may want to negotiate the proposed salary.

JOB OFFER COMPONENT CHECKLIST

Sample Pros (pluses for you)

Stable company ☐

Growth industry ☐

Global market share ☐

Like potential boss ☐

Like potential coworkers ☐

Good reputation ☐

Prospect for advancement ☐

Occasional overseas travel ☐

Signing bonus ☐

Expense account ☐

Excellent benefits ☐

Corner office/two windows ☐

Patriotic ☐

Same political persuasion as me ☐

Your personal pros from the job:

_____ ☐

_____ ☐

_____ ☐

_____ ☐

_____ ☐

_____ ☐

_____ ☐

_____ ☐

Sample Cons (negatives for you)

Base salary too low ☐

Possible future relocation(s) ☐

No company car ☐

Low monthly car allowance ☐

Lengthy commute each way ☐

60–70% road travel on the job ☐

Only one week vacation first year ☐

Move to new location ☐

Draw against commission after 90 days ☐

Your personal cons from the job:

_____

_____

_____

_____

_____

_____

_____

_____

Sample deal breakers/killers (from the cons)

Possible future relocation

45-minute commute each way

YOUR ANALYSIS OF JOB OFFER

Sample Conclusion

90-minute daily commute and extensive travel using personal car make it a no-go at any salary!

OR . . .

Salary good but politically not aligned with me.

OR . . .

GREAT opportunity in home town. Starting salary adequate with potential for bonuses and raises.

YOUR CONCLUSION =

_____

_____

_____

_____

_____

_____

_____

_____

_____

_____

_____

_____

_____

_____

_____

CLOSING THOUGHTS

I'm glad you chose TheHireAdvantage™ to learn a proven method of conducting a strategic job search instead of relying on an outdated, traditional job search everyone uses that is clearly no longer effective in today's new economy.

I have provided you with a lot of very valuable information, including the tools and resources that you need to conduct a successful search. Now it's up to you to mix and match them to best fit your needs. As you do this, make sure you customize your approach so that everything you present to a potential hiring manager is a true reflection of who you are and the value you offer.

Remember your value as your career progresses, and continue to reinvent yourself. Understand what it is you offer the business community and learn to adjust to a global economy that can affect your employment at any time. It's important that, even while employed, you continue to build your professional network and explore other opportunities. Remember, you're a professional first and someone else's employee second.

You'll find TheHireChallenge™ will continue to be a valuable resource as your career moves forward. The strategies I've introduced will provide you with the direction for success when you **again** find yourself in transition, and faced with the key challenge of **differentiation.**

Limits of Liability and Disclaimers of Warranties
Results, Earnings and Income Disclaimers

The material in this book is provided as is and without any kind of express or implied warranties. We make no guarantees that you will achieve any results from applying the author's ideas, strategies, and tactics found in this book. Because the book is a general educational information product, it is not a substitute for professional advice on the topics presented or discussed herein.

The author does not warrant or make any representations regarding the use or the results of the use of the materials in this book in terms of their correctness, accuracy, reliability, or otherwise. We make no earnings projections, promises, or representations of any kind.

The author and the publisher do not warrant this book is free from defects or that any such defects will be corrected. We further do not assume liability for nor warrant or guarantee websites, devices, or other delivery systems related to this book are free from viruses or other malware.

The author and the publisher assume no responsibility for any losses or damages resulting from your use of any link, information, or opportunity contained in this book or within any other information disclosed by the author or the publisher in any form whatsoever.

You agree to hold the author and the publisher of this book, principals, agents, affiliates, associates, and employees harmless from any and all liability for all claims for damages, including attorney's fees and costs, incurred by you or caused to third parties by you, arising out of the use or application of products, services, and activities discussed in this book. Further, the author and/or publisher are not liable for any damages that result from the use or the inability to use the information in this book even if the author, the publisher or an authorized representative has been made aware of the possibility of such damages. Should compensation be awarded for damages, losses, and causes of action (whether contract or tort including but not limited to negligence), the total awards, penalties, and costs shall not exceed the amount paid by you, if any, for this book.

You should always conduct your own investigation (perform due diligence) before implementing strategies and tactics mentioned in this book or buying products or services from anyone, be it offline or via the Internet, including products and services sold via hyperlinks embedded in this book.

Due Diligence

You are advised to perform your own due diligence when it comes to making any decisions. Use caution and seek the advice of qualified professional before acting upon the contents of this book or any other information related to its use. You shall not consider any explanations, presentations, examples, documents, or other content in this book or otherwise provided by the author or publisher using means such as but not limited to webinars or conferences, to be the equivalent of professional advice.

The author and the publisher assume no responsibility for any losses or damages resulting from your use of any link, information, or opportunity contained in this book or within any other information disclosed by the author or the publisher in any form whatsoever.

Affiliate Compensation & Connections Disclosure

Any recommended products or services mentioned in this book are based on the author's belief that the purchase of such products and services will help the readers in general or specific to the topic of this book. However, the reader is assumed to have performed their own due diligence prior to making any such purchases of a product or service mentioned in this book.

This book contains hyperlinks to websites and information created and maintained by other individuals and organizations (third parties) in addition to those owned or operated by the author and/or the publisher. The author and the publisher do not control or guarantee the accuracy, relevance, or timeliness of any information or privacy policies posted on these outside, third-party websites.

Some third parties may have a material connection to the author and/or publisher. Such third parties to hereafter be known individually and collectively as the affiliate. Because of the potential for a material connection, the reader is to always assume that the author and/or publisher may be biased because of the affiliate's relationship with the author and/or publisher and/or because the affiliate has offered or will provide something of value or compensation.

The type of compensation received by the affiliate will vary. In some instances the affiliate may provide products or services for review or use or may provide other compensation. The affiliate may further provide monetary or nonmonetary compensation to the author and/or publisher when you take an action by clicking a hyperlink in this book or make a purchase.

Purchase Price

Although the publisher believes the price is fair for the value you receive, you understand and agree the purchase price for this book has been arbitrarily set by the publisher and has no relationship to value, guarantees, or objective standards.

THEHIREROAD™ JOB SEARCH SYSTEM

I know some of you may need more help than just this book. So if you are serious about changing your mindset and implementing the tactics I've described in this book then TheHireRoad™ job-search tutorial may be your answer. In addition to showing you how to prepare the critical new tool of a biography, the program introduces other innovative tactics and strategies such as management endorsements, the post-interview packet, and the 80+ question audio interview CD, all to help you stand head and shoulders above your competition!

Get templates and samples of biographies and the necessary professionally-written resumes and cover letters.

To learn more visit http://www.TheHireChallenge.com.

APPENDIX

Glossary

Job hunting has its own language. Here are some of the terms you may hear in your job search:

Fiduciary Responsibility—The legal requirement that a company and its management first meet the needs of investors for profitability of their bonds and stocks. That means if a company can make more money for the stockholders by downsizing or outsourcing, they have a legal obligation to consider doing so. Employers generally have NO fiduciary responsibility to their employees to maintain their jobs other than contractual requirements. This is why companies do NOT want to hire employees.

Hiring Manager—An individual who will actually be in your chain of command. These are the employees such as your direct supervisor or the department head. These are the individuals who actually KNOW what the job requirements must be and have the flexibility to recognize what skills and value you may bring to the position beyond bland and meaningless keywords. Your goal is interaction with the hiring manager, NOT human resources.

Keywords—Used for search engine optimization (SEO) and sorting through large amounts of data. Keywords are used to find information on the Internet and many career sites require you to select one or more keywords to search for jobs. Many sites also ask you to provide your own keywords as part of uploading your resume.

Keywords for job searches are words that describe a job, skills, or qualification. For example, "engineering" or "hospitality" are single critical keywords that describe a job or skill as well as industry. Single critical keywords are usually combined into longtail keyword phrases like "oil field engineering" or "casino and gaming hospitality." Failure to have these keywords and phrases in your resume means you will be rejected by any organization using an online screening program.

Meatgrinder—A computer program that scans resumes and applications for keywords and phrases. The bigger the company the more likely they are to require you to complete the application online and/or upload your resume to a website for review. Your materials will then be reviewed by a computer program or by an outside HR service that has been told what keywords and phrases best represent what the employer is looking for.

Social Media—Online chat and connection sites. For job applicants, LinkedIn is the recognized leader in job searches. However, do not overlook reaching out using sites like Google+, Facebook, Twitter, and specialty sites for your industry. Equally, make sure you have removed anything questionable from your site—both your postings and friends—that may reflect badly on you should a prospective employer do a Google search on you as part of the hiring process.

NOTES

NOTES

NOTES